The
Last
Buffalo

The Last Buffalo

Walter Potts and the
92nd "Buffalo" Division
in World War I

E. B. Hogan

EAKIN PRESS ⚑ Fort Worth, Texas
www.EakinPress.com

Copyright © 2000
By E. B. Hogan
Published By Eakin Press
An Imprint of Wild Horse Media Group
P.O. Box 331779
Fort Worth, Texas 76163
1-817-344-7036
www.EakinPress.com
ALL RIGHTS RESERVED
1 2 3 4 5 6 7 8 9
ISBN-10: 1-68179-045-9
ISBN-13: 978-1-68179-045-9

Library of Congress Cataloging-in-Publication Data

Hogan, E. B.
    The last buffalo : Walter Potts and the 92nd "Buffalo" Division in WWI
/ by E. B. Hogan.
        p.   cm.
    Includes bibliographical references (p.) and index.
    ISBN 1-68179-045-9
        1. Potts, Walter Edward, 1892-1997. 2. United States. Army.
Infantry Division, 92nd. 3. World War, 1914-1918--Participation, Afro-
American. 4. Afro-American soldiers--Biography. 5. United States. Army--
Biography. 6. World War, 1914-1918--Regimental histories—United
States. I. Title.

    D639.N4 H64 2000
    940.4'03--dc21   99-049608

Grateful acknowledgment is made to the
Still Picture Branch, Nontextual Division,
of the National Archives for the permission to
reproduce the military photographs.
All other photographs are from the author's collection.

Walter E. Potts, circa 1918.

Contents

Acknowledgments

The production of this book closely embraced a lot of people. It was amazing to learn how much people care. Many people worked on their own time exclusively for the pleasure of being helpful to me. I am deeply indebted to them. One person alone cannot be singled out for willingly offering time, expertise, and insights in support of this book. I owe an unrepayable debt to my entire family. Thank you for having faith in me.

Thanks also to B. Michael Berger, director, Records Management Service, Department of Veterans Affairs; Commander Carlton G. Philpot, chairman, Buffalo Soldier Monument Committee; Michael Rogers, National Archives, Southeast Region; Rose M. Brown, chief, Awards Branch, Veterans Service Directorate, Department of the Army; all of the clerks at the Fannin County Courthouse; Tom Scott, director, Fannin County Historical Museum; Mary Fowler, director, Bertha Boyer Memorial Library; Emmitt Parker, Ravenna historian; Reverend Charles L. Gent, pastor, Union Baptist Church; Susan Hawkins, Tri County Genealogical Society; Paul Beck, director, Texas State Library and Archives; Mitchell Yockelson, reference archivist, National Archives; Kathryne Crews, director, Pottsboro Library; Dixie Foster and the clerks at the Denison Public Library; Barbara McKetchum, director, Bonham Public

Library; Diane Egelston, Wells Fargo Bank, Personal Growth Leave Committee; Bill Strowbridge, historian, Wells Fargo Bank Library; John J. Slonaker, chief reseacher, U.S. Army Military History Institute, Historical Reference Branch; Kenneth Bargmann, Department of Veterans Affairs; Richard J. Sommers, Ph.D., archivist historian, U.S. Army Military History Institute, Archives Branch; Dominique Darcis, Ambassade De France; Elizabeth L. Hill, chief, Still Picture Branch, Nontextual Archives Division, National Archives at College Park; Muriel Sue Parkhurst, editor, *The Torch* newspaper; Arnold Grisham, John H. Motley, Patty Cavallaro, and Chuck Lautrup.

I would like to extend a special thank you to Corine Safford, Henry L. Safford, Violet J. Garrett, G. B. Potts, Joye L. Potts, Michael L. Hogan, Sr., LaVanda J. McCrary, Walter C. Potts, III, Billy R. Potts, Janice A. Jackson, Maurice Miles, Shree Medlock, Claudia Barnes, and the many, many other people who helped.

Preface

The motivation to tell this story by writing a book seemed natural to me from the beginning. The life of Walter E. Potts touched many people in the almost 106 years he lived. His noble endeavors were a part of the courageous team of Buffalo Soldiers who served in France in World War I. He was the oldest documented Buffalo Soldier. It's exciting for me to have the opportunity to share this piece of black Americana which is so rich in history.

A study of the African American presence on America's frontier helped me discover this particular history. African American men and women have contributed to the advancement of this country in numerous fields. Their accomplishments of the past have served as a path to the future. African Americans have contributed again and again to the future of this country, in both large and small ways. The value of their offerings has at times been overlooked in the chronicles. Yet, long before Walter's birth more than a century ago, the endeavors of African Americans had begun to advance human intelligence not only in this country but throughout the entire world.

It should be made clear that this book makes no claim to be a complete account of the history of the 92nd Division. This is a brief chronicle of the 92nd Division's participation in World War I. A part of this history was written based on research from a number of books, periodicals, pamphlets, personal narratives, government publications, magazines, and newspapers. I have chosen to concentrate on positive experiences as much as possible because the small victories are important. The fact remains that many conditions of military life for the African American were inadequate.

The other part of this history is based on conversations with local octogenarians along with the memories of relatives and former family neighbors and friends. I am attesting that information received from each of these elements is, to the best of my knowledge, representative of what a person might have said or worn or done.

1

Buffalo Soldiers

To black Americans at the turn of the century, the term "Buffalo Soldiers" meant men of strength, daring, and great courage. These were men skilled in the arts of war, men of honor and patriotism imbued with pride in self and cause, men willing to defend the nation's honor with their very lives, if necessary. It seemed natural, then, that a combat division composed of black enlisted men in World War I should be named the "Buffalo Division." And so it was. Significantly, the shoulder patch worn by every Buffalo Soldier was adorned with the figure of a black buffalo.[1] The circular patch containing the black buffalo was on a drab olive background and was bordered in black. (See logo above.)

The four black Regular Army regiments were originally authorized by Congress in 1866. In the fall of 1867, Indian wars were raging on the rapidly expanding frontier. The Indian scouts lay motionless one day as they watched, from well over two miles in the distance, a cavalry unit file out in a column of two from within the tall, slowly opened gates of the U.S. Army post. Gradually, the Indians began to sense something strange about this cavalry unit. The soldiers seemed so different from those they were accustomed to fighting. The Indians then realized these men were black.

25th Infantry, Company "B" Buffalo Soldiers,
Fort Randall, Dakota Territory, 1882.

The black soldiers were from the Ninth and Tenth United States Cavalry regiments. Finding the Regular Army issue overcoats inadequate for the harsh, cold, blustery winters on the plains, the men killed buffaloes and made huge robes, some of which covered them from head to toe. To the Indians who had never seen black men, they did indeed resemble buffaloes. And they proved to be most formidable in battle.

Out of respect, the Indians dubbed them "Buffalo Soldiers." The men in the Ninth and Tenth Cavalry were proud of the comparison. They fought renegades, horse and cattle thieves, bank robbers, and marauding gangs; they protected payrolls, stagecoaches, wagon trains, mail carriers, railroad working parties, and even small towns, in times of civil conflict. Many of the permanent military posts were built by these soldiers, who spent long years of service in isolated, untamed frontier territory, sometimes serving as the only force against the enemies of law and order.[2]

An inadequate equipment supply caused failures at times. Casualties among key personnel tested the confidence and inspiration of the many who fought well. The soldiers' achievements bore a special quality. They stressed the courage, the flexibility, and the determination to fulfill their commitment. They fought to prevail in the face of adversity.

The experiment with Negro troopers launched in 1866 proved a success by any standard other than that of racial prejudice. By 1891 the combat record spoke for itself. They had fought on the plains of Kansas and in Indian Territory, in the vast expanse of West Texas and along hundreds of miles of the Rio Grande and in Mexico, in the deserts and mountains of New Mexico and Arizona, in Colorado, and finally in the rugged grandeur of the Dakotas. Few regiments could match the length and sweep of these activities.

Inevitably, there were individual failures, but one can search the dusty archives in vain for an instance where a detachment, company, battalion, or regiment bolted under fire or failed to do its duty. This in spite of the knowledge that their efforts would receive little or no attention, official or otherwise. Theirs was a record, too, built on generally second-rate equipment and the worst horse flesh in the army.

Their labors were not limited to the battlefield. They built or renovated dozens of posts, strung thousands of miles of wire, and escorted stages, trains, cattle herds, railroad crews, and surveying parties. Civil officials, particularly in Texas and New Mexico, could not have performed their duties without them. Their scouts and patrols opened new roads, mapped vast areas of uncharted country, and pinpointed for oncoming settlers the location of life-giving water.[3]

For the Buffalo Soldiers the capture and arrest of Satank, Satanta, and Big Tree added an exciting episode to the history of the regiment, but the accomplishment was more than that. The troopers had carried out their orders with a crisp coolness and disciplined restraint. A moment's loss of nerve or an instant's "trigger itch" could have launched a blood bath.

Neither had occurred, and only two maddened Kiowas had lost their lives.[4]

The activities of a few Comanches were demanding far too much time and energy, and in May General Ord decided to settle the problem once and for all. Colonel Shafter was ordered from Fort Duncan to Concho to organize an expedition for the purpose of sweeping the Staked Plains of hostile bands. Shafter was also given an additional task. The westward flow of settlement was slapping at the edges of the plains, and Shafter's orders required that he "show in detail, the resources of the country passed over, looking to its adaptability for cultivation and stock raising" and that he pay special attention to the location of bodies of water.[5]

Shafter's expedition killed but a single Indian and captured only five others. However, it had swept the plains clear of Indians and, more importantly, had provided the first thorough exploration of the Staked Plains, forever dispelling the myths and fears surrounding that heretofore mysterious and uncharted region.[6]

This task accomplished, the return to Fort Clark began. The men were soon half frozen, their clothing in tatters, and there was no escape from the bone-chilling cold. The post was a welcome sight when they arrived on December 3, 1877, and the command received one of Shafter's rare commendations:

> Officers and men were exposed to very severe weather and having only pack animals were necessarily restricted to the small allowance carried on the saddle. The country scouted in was exceedingly difficult, more so than any part of Texas, officers and men deserving great credit for the patience, fortitude and energy they exhibited on this scout, they are to be complimented on its successful issue.[7]

It was rough work for the Buffalo Soldiers. In a land of extremes, one day's march could bring searing desert heat that beat down mercilessly, provoking an aching thirst that often went unslaked for hours, while the night might well be spent in lonely vigil on a frosty mountaintop. Through it all, with little time for relaxation, to say nothing of entertainment, the troopers remained cheerful and uncomplaining.[8]

The Buffalo Soldiers continued their service in the Spanish-American War and added more honors and lustre to their colors. They were a segregated but integral part of the army. The Spanish-American War began on April 21, 1898. Sixteen regiments of black volunteers were recruited; four saw combat. Five black Americans won Congressional Medals of Honor.

At the Battle of San Juan Hill the black cavalrymen saved the day for the Rough Riders and Teddy Roosevelt. Although long left out of history texts, the part taken that day by the black cavalrymen was carefully recorded by reporters Jacob Riis and Stephen Bonsal and participating white military men, Lt. John J. Pershing and Frank Knox, a Rough Rider. Lieutenant Pershing, who led the Tenth, that day wrote:

> White regiments, black regiments, regulars, and Rough Riders, representing the young manhood of the North and South fought shoulder to shoulder, unmindful of race or color, unmindful of whether commanded by an ex-Confederate or not.
> . . . Through streams, tall grass, tropical undergrowth, under barbed wire fences and over wire entanglements, regardless of casualties up the hill to the right this gallant advance was made. . . . Once began it continued dauntless and unchecked in its steady, dogged, persistent advance until, like a mighty resistless torrent, it dashed triumphant over the crest of the hill and firing a parting volley at the vanishing foe, planted the silken standards on the enemy's breastworks, and the Stars and Stripes over the blockhouse on San Juan Hill to stay.[9]

World War I began in Europe in 1914. President Woodrow Wilson proclaimed U.S. neutrality. During the month of August 1915, the *Washington Post* and the *Baltimore Sun* carried stories stating that General Staff was planning to send a force of one million soldiers overseas. That same month the Army War College Division denied the allegations in both newspapers. In January 1916 President Wilson launched a nationwide whistle-stop campaign to generate support for preparedness and the Continental Army with three speeches in New York. By the end of the month the Army War College had warned its civilian employees to engage in no discussion whatsoever concerning the progress of the European War.

Above: *24th Infantry Buffalo Soldiers, Siboney, Cuba, 1898.*

Below: *9th Cavalry Buffalo Soldiers after the charge at San Juan Hill, Camp Wichoff, 1899.*

Above: *9th Cavalry Buffalo Soldiers in camp near Santiago, Cuba, 1898.*

Below: *25th Infantry, Company "B" Buffalo Soldiers, Fort Missoula, Montana, 1895.*

The National Defense Act on June 3 authorized a five-year expansion of the U.S. Army. At the same time it drastically limited the size and the authority of the U.S. War Department General Staff. It was not until mid-September that Newton D. Baker, U.S. secretary of war, ruled that the U.S. War Department General Staff had the authority for supervisory and planning roles.

In late December Gen. Hugh L. Scott, chief of staff to Secretary of War Baker, championed a peacetime draft in a testimony to the Senate. More than a month later Scott received a "Plan for a National Army" from the War College Division that called for a regular army of 310,000, a civilian reserve of 2,500,000, and universal military training. The Army War College Division issued an initial report to General Scott that hinted at foreign involvement of United States troops and recommended that all United States forces receive full training in America before departing. Additionally, Newton Baker asked the Division to plan to raise a force of volunteers tentatively fixed at 500,000. Baker also warned President Wilson that great suspicion would be aroused if compulsory military service were suggested at the outset before any opportunity to volunteer had been given. President Wilson then ordered Baker to draft legislation that would give the president the authority to raise, but not use, an army with the provisions for conscription, if Germany committed an overt act while Congress was not in session.

In the "Allies Appeal for American Assistance" it was the opinion of the Supreme War Council that, in order to carry the war to a successful conclusion, an American army should be formed as early as possible under its own commander and under its own flag. In order to deal with the emergency it was agreed that American troops should be sent to France as rapidly as Allied transportation facilities would permit. Preference would be given to infantry and machine-gun units for training and service with French and British armies.

One of the men sent overseas was Walter E. Potts. He obtained the distinguished rank of corporal for his service in the war. The U.S. Army discharge dated March 28, 1919, is something he would proudly display. He served with the U.S. Army 92nd Division, 367th Infantry Battalion, Company E.

Black draftees arriving at an induction center at
Camp Meade, Maryland.

When inducted into the army on October 29, 1917, Walter was a young man and in excellent physical condition. His strenuous toil as a highly skilled farmer, combined with his attitude about the war, had well prepared him. Within the solid family foundation of the elders, he shared a happy home. Traveling from Denison, he left home on October 25, 1917, en route to Camp Travis in San Antonio, Texas. He was to receive the required military training that accompanied his call to war. He remembered that three minutes before the train left Bonham for San Antonio he said, " 'If I have to die to help America, then let me die.' I felt it was my place to go. I was supposed to go. I am part of this country."

Walter later recalled World War I as if it happened yesterday. Responding to the draft notice that came in the mail, he registered on Monday, June 5, 1917. He was scared like all the young men but, he said, "I didn't question it. It was my duty to serve my country."

Because of the racial policies of the day, black soldiers

were not welcomed to fight alongside the European-American soldiers of the American Expeditionary Forces. The 369th Infantry was assigned to the French 16th Division. In action with the French, the regiment was awarded two medals of honor and many Croix de Guerre, and was considered to be one of the best decorated units of the war.

Emmett J. Scott, special assistant to Secretary of War Newton D. Baker for Negro Affairs, wrote: "When the war against Germany was declared on April 6, 1917, Negro Americans quickly recognized the fact it was not to be a white man's war, nor a black man's war, but a war of all the people living under the Stars and Stripes for the preservation of human liberty throughout the world."[10]

The draft law, passed in May 1917, required the registration of all male citizens between the ages of twenty-one and thirty-one. Both blacks and whites wondered whether Negroes, bitter from their long history of oppression, might not resist the call to fight for the white America which had oppressed them.

The postwar report of Provost Marshal General Crowder laid to rest any lingering question about the response of blacks. The evidence is conclusive that the Negro's response to America's call in times of world war will remain a lasting tribute to his patriotism. He furnished his quota cheerfully. As Charles Williams commented, "The doubts expressed of his Americanism were ill considered and the fears concerning his loyalty were groundless."[11]

The response was not quite so unanimously enthusiastic as General Crowder stated, but in general he was right. One captain, about to set sail for France, expressed the hope in the heart of every Negro when he said: "I am leaving today a wife and three children. As great as the sacrifice is, I shall be satisfied never to see America again, if my wife and children will share greater opportunities and enjoy more liberty than I now enjoy"; and not only the men but the women who saw them leave shared this point of view.[12]

When World War I began, blacks in uniform numbered some 20,000. The number drafted was 367,710 blacks. During World War I, 140,000 blacks were in France; 40,000 of them saw actual combat.[13]

The 92nd Division was organized, beginning October 26, 1917, by detachments, in cantonments that were widely separated, geographically. In the latter part of May and the first part of June 1918, the division was partially assembled at Camp Upton, Long Island, New York, for purposes of embarkation only. This is the only approach to an assembly of the division in the United States. Since there was a wide geographical dispersion of the detachments during organization, their training was conducted under varying conditions.

No information has been found in regard to the instruction of the division as a whole, and there is a dearth of such records as weekly drill schedules and similar papers. The reports of inspectors general on inspections of the different detachments, and the remarks on monthly returns, are the chief sources of information.

The report of an inspection by an inspector general dated February 12, 1918, made January 30 to February 5, 1918, did not specifically mention training of the 92nd Division units. However, the following remark of the inspector appears to cover all organizations at the cantonment:

> It is not contended that too little time has been given to fundamental infantry training, but it is believed that not sufficient attention has been given to precision in the details of training. Neither officers nor noncommissioned officers have been required to learn with exactitude the provisions of the Drill Regulations and Manual of Interior Guard, which are used daily in the instruction of the men.

The course of instruction outlined by headquarters at Camp Grant in January 1918 included: physical training, drill for precision and snap, bombing, moving picture instruction, bayonet training, occupation of trench area, target practice or practice march, and transportation lecture.

A report of the 86th Division inspector to the division commander, dated December 14, 1917, contains the following:

> Any report concerning methods and results of training in this Division must take into consideration certain factors that affect seriously the progress of that training and thus diminish the results that might otherwise be expected. The lack of

proper equipment has been and continues to be the most serious handicap to instruction. Inclement weather threatens to preclude any outdoor instruction for several weeks to come. . .

A recapitulation of the conditions will show the many divergent and conflicting elements that entered into the training of the 92nd Division. The quota of the draft from which the 92nd Division drew the bulk of its enlisted personnel was late in being called to service. The first return rendered by this division was dated November 30, 1917. Although, at that time, the division as a whole numbered 846 officers and 15,821 enlisted men, some units were late in being organized. Naturally, this shortened the training period. The most glaring example of this was the 317th Trench Mortar Battery that, according to the monthly return, was organized May 20, 1918. On June 26, 1918, it joined the American Expeditionary Forces in France. Another factor that unduly shortened the training period, particularly the outdoor portion of it, was the rigor of the climate, as all detachments were located in northern or cold zones.

2

Journey of Honor

The training of a division in France was intended to cover about ninety days, split into three phases. The first phase included the instruction of small units; the second was training in line, preferably in a quiet sector, brigaded with an older unit; the third was work in a training area, correcting deficiencies discovered, and training the division as a whole, primarily in open warfare.

The first four divisions to arrive in France had a distinct advantage over all others. They went through all phases of the training and, since they were the laboratory material used in the experimental determination of the programs for the others, had much more than the regulation amount of time. Even among these, however, there were great differences, and the 1st Division was the only one that had its third phase in full.

The first unit of the 92nd Division arrived in France on June 16, 1918. The last unit arrived on July 13, 1918. Division headquarters was established June 29, 1918, at Bourbonne-les-Bains (Haute Marne) in the 11th Training Area. About July 6, 1918, training was begun, according to the

*Officers of the "Buffaloes," 367th Infantry,
77th Division in France, 1918.*

"General Principles Governing the Training of Units of the
American Expeditionary Forces." On August 11, 1918, the division moved to Brouvelieures (Vosges). On August 23, 1918,
it moved to St. Die and began entering the line in the Vosges,
east and north of St. Die, being associated with French units,
for training. It took over the sector on its own responsibility
August 31, 1918.

The 92nd Division's advance detachment reached Brest,
June 18, 1918, and moved to Bourbonne-les-Bains June 26,
1918. Reaching France by way of England, the artillery, after
spending from July 1, 1918, to August 12, 1918, at Montmo-
rillon (Vienne), went to La Courtine (Creuse), where it received
the standard course of instruction until the latter part of October 1918, when it joined the division in the Marbache
sector.

The infantry was fortunate that during the training period all elements of the division essential to infantry training were concentrated in the 11th Training Area, under the control of the division commander. However, there were certain conditions, beyond the control of the division, which were detrimental to its training.

On June 28, 1918, about 50 percent of the troops were in the training area. The remainder were coming in rapidly but were deficient in equipment. For example: they had no transportation, kitchens, machine guns, automatic rifles, pistols, 1-pounder guns, Stokes mortars, or grenades, and had only 100 rounds of rifle ammunition. On July 18, 1918, the machine gun battalions were still deficient in equipment, such as pistols, range finders, prismatic and Brunton compasses, protractors, angle of site instruments, clinometers, projectors, flag kits for wigwag, transportation, live grenades, box respirators, and target material. Also, the machine gun battalions had not received machine gun tripods, although they were entering their second week of training. There were no animals in the training area with the division until July 25, 1918, when twenty-eight horses and six mules were received.

In addition to disciplinary and hygienic subjects, training included the following:

training of bombers	musketry behind the lines
map reading	instruction in the use of
location by coordinates	field glasses
patrolling	compass reading
scouting	front line intelligence
instruction of runners	dugouts and demolition
gathering and transmitting	sniping
information	estimating distances
indication of targets	combat signals
verbal and written messages	rifle and pistol practice with
counterattack	gas masks on
gas instruction	and bayonet instruction.

On September 20, 1918, the 92nd Division was relieved from the St. Die sector and proceeded by road and rail to the 1st Army Corps Area. On the same day, the 368th Infantry was detached and placed at the disposal of the French 38th Corps to act as combat liaison on the left of the American First Army. The artillery was still absent in training. With these exceptions, all units of the division were present.

September 24, division headquarters opened at Beauchamp Farm in the 1st Corps Area, a little over 2.5 kilometers southwest of Clermont en Argonne, Meuse. The concentration of troops was complete by September 25. On that date, the division constituted the reserve of the 1st Corps and was assembled in the woods northwest of Clermont en Argonne, prepared to move forward at one hour's notice. On September 26 the 317th Engineers, with three battalions of infantry attached, were placed at the disposal of the corps engineers for the purpose of building passageways over "no man's land." This day the 1st Corps initiated its attack at the left of the First Army, in the Meuse-Argonne Operation.

By verbal order of the commanding general, 1st Corps, at 12:35 P.M., September 29, the division was placed at the disposal of the French 38th Corps. At this time another unit was detached from the division, namely the 183rd Brigade, less the three battalions with the engineers. These battalions and the engineers continued to remain with the corps engineers. This left under the division commander only one regiment of one brigade and three battalions of the other; the machine gun battalions, less two companies; the trains; the military police, less a small detachment; and the field signal battalion. All detachments continued to be supplied from the division. On September 30, the elements of the division with the French were regrouped in the vicinity of St. Menehould. At 3:00 P.M. the same day, the division command post passed from Beauchamp Farm to St. Menehould.

The French 1st Dismounted Cavalry Division was operating on the right bank of the Aisne, attacking in the direction of Grand Pre. Its objective was the capture of the hills south of that town. The French corps commander intended to relieve the French division with the 92nd. Therefore, he directed that the 92nd be held immediately in rear of the French division. Reconnaissance was made by the 92nd, with a view to selecting an advanced command post and effecting the relief. It was

367th Machine Gun Company, passing through town en route to the front. St. Menehould, France, September 1918.

intended by the French corps commanders that this portion of the line should pass to the command of the 92nd at 8:00 A.M., October 2. However, the day before, on October 1, his plans changed and the original order directing the relief was revoked.

On October 3 the 92nd was put at the disposal of the American First Army and ordered from St. Menehould to the Passavant region. Thus, opportunity to enter the line in this sector under the French was closed. The division command post was established at Passavant en Argonne at 6:00 P.M. on October 4.

At 11:00 P.M., October 4, the First Army issued an order directing the division, less artillery and engineers, to proceed by rail to the 4th Corps Area, and to detrain in the region of Belleville. The 92nd detrained at Frouard, Jarville, and Champigneulles, then moved by road to the 4th Corps Area, where it proceeded to the occupation of the Marbache sector, establishing headquarters at Jaillon on October 6. On October 10 the Marbache sector was completely occupied by the 92nd with headquarters at Marbache.

Consideration should be given to the nature of the terrain over which this group was about to operate. During a special investigation regarding the action of the 368th Infantry, in his testimony before the inspector general, Col. Fred H. Brown, the regimental commander said,

> It was a terrible job getting thru that Boch wire. There were two or three kilometers of solid mass of French and German wire in "No Man's Land," and thruout the German trench system which they had been working on for four years, and the whole country except in the bayous (sic) and trenches was covered with this mass of barb wire and covered with second growth brush. The new growth had grown up through this barb wire and was absolutely impenetrable. After they got beyond the ravine Metruese it opened out a little bit and they were able to progress other than in bayous. The position had been held by both the French and Germans for the entire war, and had been constantly improved by both sides. It consisted of a rolling country cut up by ravines and covered with the ruined debris of the Argonne Forest blasted away by four years of shell fire and interlaced by solid wire defenses of every kind, it was generally considered as one of the strongest parts of the Hindenburg line especially because of the fact that this wire had not been destroyed by shell fire or tank or any similar means.

The 365th, 366th, 367th, and 368th infantry regiments were designated the core of the 92nd Division. Due to the fear of having too many black soldiers in any one place in the country, the 92nd Division was scattered out in seven different locations across the nation. It never came together as a division until one brief moment in France. Even then, its core units were assigned to the French 2nd and 4th armies. They fought alongside French soldiers, under the French command, using French weapons and equipment.

Nevertheless, the units of this division compiled an excellent combat record, in both valor and objectives achieved. Most of its officers were black.

Combat units of this black division consisted of two brigades, four infantry regiments, three field artillery regiments, one engineer regiment, three machine gun battalions, one field signal battalion, one supply train, and one military police unit.

Initial acknowledgment on the performance of black soldiers in World War I was full of praise and glory. However, as the records of performance of these soldiers were taken as the basis for what use to make of blacks in the event of another war, many of those who had given the blacks glowing reports changed their opinions. The record, however, stands for itself.[14]

Despite the limitations suffered in civilian life and in the army, Negro individuals and units distinguished themselves. Pvt. Henry Johnson and Pvt. Needham Roberts of the 369th Infantry put to flight a German raiding party. For this heroism, they were awarded France's Croix de Guerre, and were widely publicized in news media in the U.S. The French Croix de Guerre was awarded to three Negro regiments of the 93rd Infantry Division, to a company of the fourth regiment, and to the 1st Battalion of the 367th Infantry, 92nd Infantry Division.[15]

The 367th Infantry Regiment, 92nd Division, was organized on November 3, 1917, at Camp Upton, New York. The action was in response to orders from the headquarters of the 17th Division. Moving to Hoboken, New Jersey, on June 8, 1918, the regiment sailed on the USS *America* for France on June 10, 1918.[16]

Maj. Gen. Charles C. Ballou was appointed to command the division in the order directing its organization. He did not have an opportunity to study conditions in France prior to arriving there with his division. Although he did make repeated attempts to concentrate his division in one cantonment, it was never mobilized and trained as a division in the United States, but was scattered in detachments, varying in size, over seven cantonments extending from Kansas to New York. This resulted in: (a) the detachments being organized and trained under the supervision of seven different local commanders who

*Maj. Gen.
Charles C.
Ballou, 92nd
Division
commander.*

formed no part of the division and whose connection to it was
purely temporary; (b) the personal influence and control of the
division commander being limited to written communications
and occasional personal inspections; and (c) difference in climatic conditions, issues of clothing and equipment, discipline,
morale, and progress, type and characteristics of training.

From date of organization to date of embarkation, the
strength of the division fluctuated constantly. A check of the
divisional returns for this period shows certain inaccuracies.
There were monthly gains and losses. The commissioned personnel varied from approximately sixty-nine officers short to
forty-six officers over and above the authorized strength. The
enlisted personnel were always short, varying from approxi-

mately 15,943 in November 1917 to 25,255 in June 1918, the month the division embarked.

The commanding general of the 92nd Division, Charles Ballou, insisted that some blacks, though "in no great numbers," could become competent officers, and he objected to lowering standards in order to obtain the desired 1,250 black officer trainees. The 92nd Division, which he had so confidently taken overseas, might have lived up to his expectations, he believed, if the army had stressed quality rather than numbers in commissioning blacks and assigned white officers not poisoned by racial prejudice.[17]

Although a certain amount of discipline was instilled in the division, only rudimentary training was given in the United States because of the following: bulk of the personnel, low strength, fluctuations in strength, large number of recruits received just prior to embarking, lack of proper equipment, impossibility of central control, adverse climatic conditions, and shortness of the training period.

Non-white soldiers served in the Great War from the very beginning, because all the major powers used troops from their colonies in Africa and Asia. A number of black men held high command in the French Army, and at least two were generals.

Respect for the American troops was acknowledged in a message prepared on June 2, 1918, by the prime ministers of Great Britain, France, and Italy stating:

> We desire to express our warmest appreciation to President Wilson for the remarkable promptness with which American aid, in excess of what at one time seemed practicable, has been rendered to the Allies during the past month to meet a great emergency. The crisis, however, still continues. General Foch has presented to us a statement of the utmost gravity, which points out that the numerical superiority of the enemy in France, where 162 Allied divisions now oppose 200 German divisions, is very heavy, and that, as there is no possibility of the British and French increasing the number of their divisions here is a great danger of the war being lost unless the numerical inferiority of the Allies can be remedied as rapidly as possible by the advent of American troops. In addition, looking to the future, it is impossible to foresee ultimate victory in the war unless America is able to provide

367th Infantry orders.

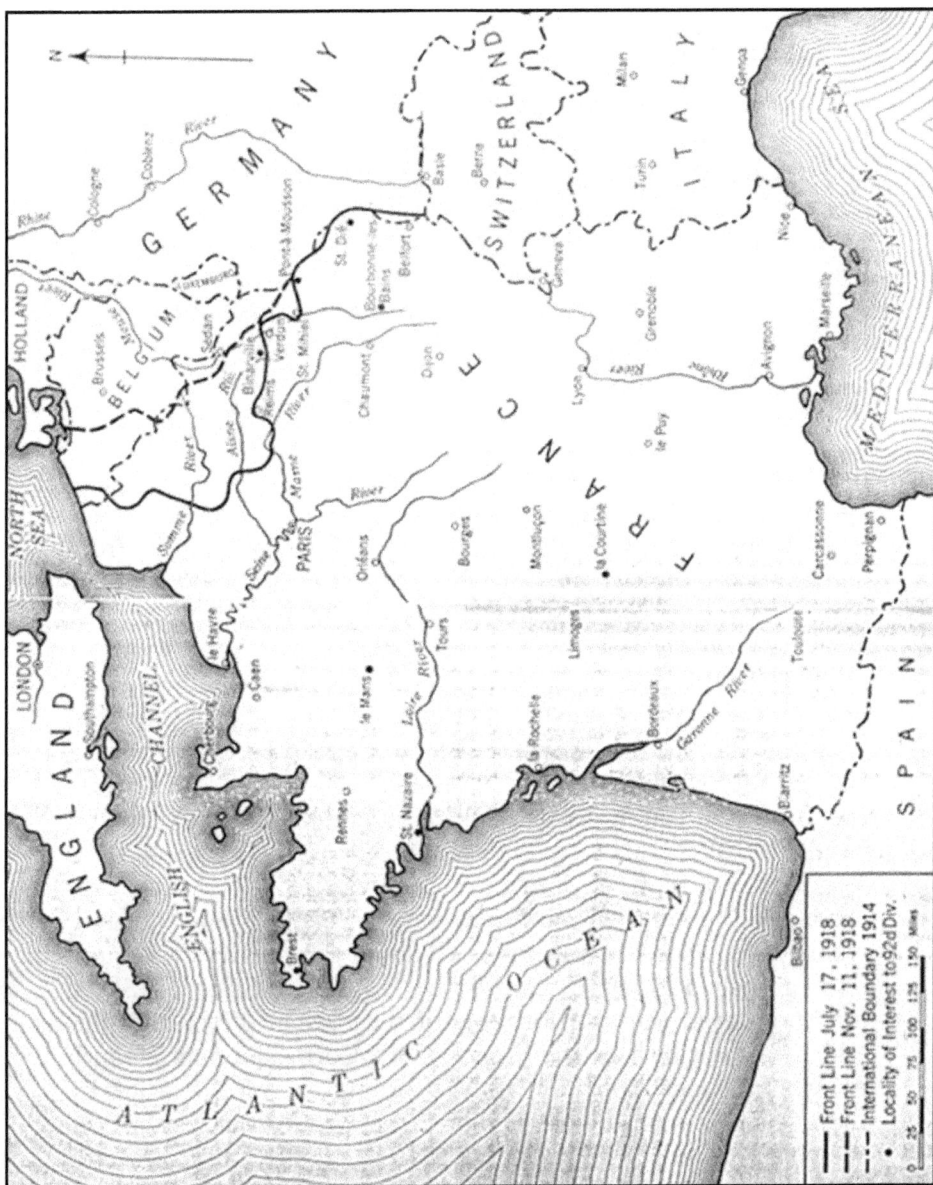

WWI
American
forces front
line
operations
map.

such an army as will enable the Allies ultimately to establish numerical superiority.

Walter Potts left the shores of the United States on board the USS *America* on June 10, 1918. The regiment sailed for France on a voyage to engage in battle on the front lines of the Great War. This was his chance to practice staying alive. Some of the time was spent singing battle hymns, such as "The Fight is On." There was one woman, a Red Cross nurse, onboard the ship, along with more than 1,100 men. Additionally there were six German engineers onboard. The voyage lasted nine days.

Walter was sent to France to help near Metz, Germany. At times he was stationed about 700 yards from the German lines on the border between France and Germany. He recalled that they were shelled "Every night after nine. We had to hold a trench line for eighteen days and nights, and we did. And every night after nine you knew someone was going to die from German one-pound artillery shells. For three hours a night they would try to get us with shells that exploded about four feet over the ground." After hiking 160 miles to the front, the men existed on "hardtack," biscuits that had to be soaked in water before they were edible. "Lots of guys fell out, just blacked out from the march," Walter said. The men would be better able to successfully survive other long hikes once they had completed the intensive training course in the vital elements of combat.

The 367th Infantry, 184th Infantry Brigade, 92nd Division, arrived at Brest (Finistere) on June 19, 1918, and proceeded to the area around Bourbonne les Bains (Haute Marne), where it remained in training until about the middle of August. Then it began a move toward the front. On August 23 the 367th entered the division area of the French 87th Division, which formed part of the French 33rd Corps, French Seventh Army. On August 29 the regiment formed part of the relief, by the 92nd Division, of the French 87th Division in the St. Die sector (Lorraine). The regiment served actively in this sector until September 20. The regiment was credited for battle participation in the St. Die sector (Lorraine) from August 23 to September 20, 1918.[18]

On August 31 the Germans attacked in an attempt to recapture the village of Frappelle. Their attack was supported by intense artillery bombardment, mustard gas, and flame throwers, but they were repulsed with heavy losses.

Early on the morning of September 12 the 367th Infantry Regiment was bombarded with what at first was thought to be gas shells. After only moments, a closer inspection of the "shells" revealed that they were circulars of printed matter. These circulars were intended to destroy the enthusiastic desire of the black soldiers to fight for the United States. The propaganda material suggested that the soldiers throw their weapons away and go over to the German lines. It asked the soldiers to question democracy and the personal freedom of the Negro in America. Fine positions in business in Berlin and other German cities were promised. The discovery of true friendship and having Germans as real friends was also promised in the circulars.

To the honor and recognition of those thousands of Negro officers and men, the invitation had no effect other than to give a personal view of the German methods and to inspire in them a grander image of their duty to the United States.

Periodic bombardments of the circulars continued until the 367th was relieved from the St. Die sector along with the 92nd Division on September 20. During the four weeks the division had held this sector, all attacks had been repulsed and quantities of material had been captured.

Upon leaving the St. Die sector (Lorraine), the 367th Infantry proceeded to the area of the American 1st Army Corps. On September 25 the 92nd Division constituted corps reserve of the American 1st Army Corps, and the 367th Infantry entered the corps area on September 26, entering the line on the same date. On September 30 this regiment passed to the command of the French 38th Army Corps. The regiment served actively in the Meuse Argonne operation until October 5. The regiment was credited for battle participation in the Meuse Argonne from September 26 to October 5, 1918.[19]

From October 1 through October 3 the 92nd Division was in reserve with the 1st Dismounted French Cavalry Division. On October 5 the division was withdrawn from the Argonne sector and ordered to the Marbache sector northwest of Nancy. The 367th Infantry entered the Marbache sector (Lor-

Above: *367th Infantry, en route to Marbache, Belleville Meuse, France, October 12, 1918.*

Below: *369th Infantry in the trenches on the front lines in France near Maffrecourt in the Argonne region, May 4, 1918.*

Above: *365th Infantry blacksmith and a view of the blacksmith shop, Sergieux, Haute Marne, France, August 11, 1918.*

Below: *92nd Division soldiers in France.*

raine) on October 9, taking part in the relief by the 92nd Division of the French 69th Division. The 367th Infantry relieved the 56th Infantry when the American 6th Army Corps extended its zone limits. The regiment entered the line on October 26 and served actively until the armistice. Battle participation for the regiment in the Marbache sector (Lorraine) ran from October 9 to November 11, 1918.[20]

On October 10 and 11, 1918, the division attacked with the 2nd Army and occupied the Bios Cheminot, the Bois de la Voivrotte, and Bois Frehaut. In the last attack on November 10, the 367th Infantry was attacking in a column of battalions and maintaining close contact with the units on its left. The attack started at 7:00 A.M. and continued until about 9:30, when a unit adjacent to the 367th was held up by murderous machine gun fire covering the enemy's barbed wire entanglements. The 1st Battalion of the 367th Infantry and the Regimental Machine Gun Company, along with a company from the 350th Machine Gun Battalion, held the Germans at bay, silenced their machine guns, and permitted the unit to withdraw. For this action the French commanding officer under whom the rescued unit was brigaded cited the battalion and the machine gun companies. In this action the regiment lived up to its motto of "See It Through."[21]

The 367th was composed mostly of New York draftees and had as its commander Col. James A. Moss, a Southerner of long experience with black troops. He called his regiment the Buffaloes, the name given many years before by the Indians to the black regulars and later adopted by the entire 92nd Division. Of Moss's 108 officers, only eight were white, and most were from New York.[22]

Sixty percent of the soldiers who composed the 367th Infantry Regiment were from the state of New York; the South furnished twenty percent, while the remainder came from New England and the West. Commander Colonel Moss, originally from Louisiana and an authority on military tactics, has published several books on the subject.[23]

OFFICERS OF THE 367TH

Col. Erskine B. Bassett	Maj. Henry H. Arnold
Lt. Col. William G. Doane	Maj. Wilford Twyman

Lt. Col. Max A. Elser
Lt. Col. Thomas A. Rothwell
Maj. Charles L. Mitchel
Maj. Fred W. Bugbee
Maj. William H. Edwards

Maj. Charles L. Appleton
Maj. Fitztingo L. Minnegorode
Maj. Harry C. Bartlett
Maj. Ray D. Dillon
Capt. Frederick Bull

BLACK OFFICERS

Capt. Peter McCall
Capt. Robert B. Chubb
Capt. Charles Garvin
Chaplain L. H. Hamilton
1st Lt. Charles Lane
1st Lt. J. H. N. Waring
1st Lt. H. J. W. Clifford

1st Lt. Almando Henderson
2nd Lt. R. D. Hardeway
2nd Lt. E. P. Sawyer
2nd Lt. R. W. Fearing
Lt. E. B. Williams
Lt. Thomas J. Bullock

OFFICERS OF THE 92nd DIVISION
Division Commanders

Brig. Gen. Charles C. Ballou
Brig. Gen. John E. McMahon
Brig. Gen. Malvern-Hill Barnum

Maj. Gen. Charles H. Martin
Brig. Gen. James B. Erwin

183rd Infantry Brigade Commanders

Brig. Gen. Malvern-Hill Barnum
Col. Ralph B. Parrott

Brig. Gen. Charles Gerhardt

184th Infantry Brigade Commanders

Brig. Gen. William H. Hay
Col. James A. Moss
Col. Fred R. Brown

Brig. Gen. Albert H. Blanding
Col. Erskine B. Bassett

167th Field Artillery Brigade Commanders

Brig. Gen. John E. McMahon
Col. Fred T. Austin
Col. Dan T. Moore

Col. William E. Cole
Brig. Gen. John H. Sherburne
Col. Wade H. Carpenter

Chiefs of Staff

(November 1917)
Lt. Col. Allen J. Greer
(July 1918)
Lt. Col. James P. Barney, Jr.

(August 1918)
Lt. Col. Allen J. Greer
(December 1918)
Col. George K. Wilson

The infantry regiments were probably the best known, not only among the Negro people but in army circles as well.

Negroes had made a glorious record in this branch of the service and were naturally expected to defend that record. The thousands of soldiers inducted into the division, and especially those drawn to the four infantry regiments, began their training resolved that they would live up to the traditions of the past. The men were fully conscious of their responsibility and began their work with enthusiasm. So well did black soldiers absorb this training that they were often considered the best drilled and best disciplined organizations in the camps where they trained. This was said to be true of the 367th Infantry, known as the "Buffaloes," who trained at Camp Upton.[24] Gen. George Bell called the 367th the best drilled regiment in the camp and told the men he could lead them with complete confidence against any soldiers in the world.[25]

Walter Potts later said he knew what waiting was like on the front lines and had a deep feeling for the men and women "over there" in subsequent years. Tears filled his eyes as he talked of the world's plight in the Persian Gulf and of the men and women who would lose their lives. "And for what? . . . only a piece of land, just like in World War I," he said.

About his tour he said, "We lost 13 of our 500 men the first night there from machine gun fire. We were better soldiers after that. At one time my job was to signal the French guns with rockets; red for more fire, white for range finding and blue for 'OK in here'."

A God-fearing man, Walter said the only reason he made it then and ever after was because of the Lord.

He remembered having to wear a gas mask for sixteen hours a day. And in some cases they had to manufacture their own. He said, "You would not last six hours without a gas mask."

Regarding the officers in the French Army, he said, "There were no differences made. As a matter of fact the French spoke more highly of the Americans than their own. There was no prejudice at all."

The relationship between the black soldiers, the black welfare workers, and the French people was most cordial and friendly and grew in sympathy and understanding, as their association brought about a closer acquaintance.[26] One could frequently hear the expression *"soldat noir, tres gentil, tres poli"* (black soldier very genteel, very polite). This characteristic impressed the French people.[27] The black soldiers were made welcome guests in the homes of the wealthy and cultured, as well as in the most humble. The understanding ear of the black man seemed attuned to the French language, and he learned more quickly than others, it seemed, how to converse with this romantic people. The French people are affectionate and demonstrative, which corresponds to the deep emotional spirit which seems the heritage of the black American.[28]

Walter reported that he almost never experienced any racial discrimination in the army. But he added, "Well, there was one time in the army when some whites from the Georgia Rattlesnakes unit 'acted up,' but then that didn't last long when they realized they were all there for the same reason." He remembered that the Georgia Rattlesnakes were the worst in the military. They obviously felt that discrimination against blacks was practiced in France as it was in the United States. Walter said, "Everyone (blacks) was respected as someone except in America." The men in the Georgia Rattlesnakes even frequently fought among themselves. "We came to an understanding about brotherhood and citizenship," Walter recalled. "We had to learn that soldiers were soldiers and that was all there was to it." He said that they had a different relationship from then on, and got along great.

The 368th, which with the 367th composed the 184th Brigade, had a very different provenience, consisting as it did of draftees from Tennessee, Pennsylvania, and Maryland. Col. William P. Jackson was its commander, and he had assigned to him ninety-seven black officers from Des Moines.

When some men objected to the war, their views were considered. There were 3,100 former soldiers with the 3,500 prisoners at Fort Leavenworth, Kansas, on February 1, 1918. They went into a mutiny two weeks prior to that date when 113 conscientious objectors were set free with honorable discharges and $400 in back pay. A letter from Secretary of War Newton D. Baker was addressed to the prisoners through Col. Sedgewick Rice, commandant of disciplinary barracks at Fort Leavenworth. The letter virtually promised them clemency

from their harsh war court-martial sentences. Rice assembled
the prisoners and read the letter to them:

> I have carefully considered the representations made to
> me through you by the general prisoners confined at the
> Disciplinary Barracks, Fort Leavenworth. It should be said at
> the outset that the court martial proceedings in the case of
> every one of the prisoners have been carefully examined and
> their legality approved in the office of the Judge Advocate
> General of the army. This fact, however, does not touch the
> question whether the punishment may not reasonably be
> said to have been unduly severe in the first instance or in
> any event whether in view of the changed situation it ought
> now to be reduced. I fully appreciate that the cessation of
> hostilities and the return of conditions approximating those
> of peace render it just and proper that clemency should now
> be exercised toward the prisoners convicted by general court
> martial for the offenses committed since the beginning of the
> present war.
>
> With this end in view I have, as you know, adopted a
> plan in accordance with which, so far as it concerns the dis-
> ciplinary barracks at Fort Leavenworth under your charge,
> you will report as soon as possible to the Judge Advocate
> General of the Army, and the material facts concerning each
> prisoner, pertinent to the consideration of clemency in his
> case together with your own recommendation as to the mea-
> sure of clemency to be extended. By my direction also such
> reports and recommendations from you will upon receipt in
> the office of the Judge Advocate General be given immediate
> consideration in that office in the light of all that the record
> reveals and made be the commandant of the disciplinary bar-
> racks. The Judge Advocate General, upon such considera-
> tion, will report to me and submit such recommendation to
> me for my action in each case as the dictates of justice may
> require. In this manner the promptest possible action will be
> obtained, provided, of course, that the prisoners conduct
> themselves in a disciplinary and orderly manner so as not to
> make the extension of clemency an impossibility. They ought
> to realize, I am sure, the desire of the department to deal
> fairly and justly with each one of them, and each should aid
> the department to the speediest accomplishment of its pur-
> pose.[29]

Perhaps the best of the American black units to fight the Germans, Col. William Hayward's 369th Infantry, had evolved from the 15th New York, hardly a typical National Guard outfit. Neither was Hayward an ordinary National Guard officer. He apparently respected his black troops, and in any event, he did not spare himself in looking out for them. When the regiment mustered to report for federal service, he took a turn ladling food into mess gear to make sure the men were fed. In addition, he made skillful use of his political friends in building unit morale, arranging for the governor to present the colors of the 15th New York and persuading an industrialist to buy instruments for the band.

In persuading young blacks to enter the enlisted ranks, the colonel called upon a celebrated black entertainer, Bert Williams, who had himself been a militia officer in his youth. Hayward's best recruiting tool, however, proved to be the regimental band, led by a talented black musician, James Europe, who recruited instrumentalists from as far away as Chicago.[30]

In France, after exchanging their original title of 15th New York for the designation of 369th Infantry, the "Men of Bronze," as Hayward's soldiers styled themselves, traded their equipment for French weapons and other gear and underwent a brief indoctrination in trench warfare. Like the other three regiments of the provisional division, the New Yorkers served as a component of the armies of France.

News of the armistice found the 367th and the 366th more than a kilometer in advance of their position of the day before when the attack had begun; the 365th had pushed ahead about three kilometers. All had reached their objectives, but at the heavy cost of about 500 casualties.

In the 367th, Maj. Charles Appleton's 1st Battalion was sent in to help the 7th Division (white), whose attack had failed, and the French 56th Infantry, which was pinned down by heavy fire. Through the force of an assault by the black troops on the enemy flank, the French were able to withdraw and reform. For this, Major Appleton's battalion was awarded a unit Croix de Guerre. The Buffaloes had made good.[31]

The *Congressional Record* of February 28, 1919, contains the following statement concerning the 1st Battalion of the

367th Infantry of the 92nd Division: "The entire first battalion of the three hundred and sixty-seventh (Buffaloes) Infantry was cited for bravery, and awarded the Croix de Guerre, thus entitling every officer and man in the battalion to wear this distinguished French decoration. This citation was made by the French Commission because of the splendid service and bravery shown by this battalion in the last engagement of the war." The writer has been unable to find a copy of the citation in the War Department records; but because it did appear in the *Congressional Record* as indicated and also given publicity in the newspapers of the country, it is included in the story of the 92nd Division.[32]

On November 10, 1918, the 33rd Division reached the Bois d'Harville, east of the Mozelle River, and took Marcheville, but the Germans counterattacked and forced the Americans to withdraw in what was no mere rearguard action. The 7th Division held a hill despite counterattack, while the 92nd took the Bois Frehaut, just east of the Moselle. In Flanders, two American divisions attached to the French Sixth Army moved across the Belgian border despite intense fire and crossed the Escaut. In his diary General Bullard noted coldly that his divisions "found the enemy everywhere" and "fought at it all day."[33]

The entire regiment was awarded the Croix de Guerre for the taking of Sechault. The 369th was the regiment that most impressed and pleased the French. One thing that gave them particular pleasure was that many of the black troops had learned to speak French. Secretary Baker was reported to have called the 369th the all-around most serviceable regiment sent to France.[34]

The recommendation for this citation was made by General LeBouc, with the approval of General Gouraud, Marshal Petain, and General Pershing. One hundred and sixty-seven officers and men received decorations, including the Congressional Medal of Honor, the Distinguished Service Cross, the Croix de Guerre, and the Legion of Honor.[35]

Walter remembered that the men in his unit were ordered to march seven miles to Metz across a line the Kaiser had said no man would ever cross. "That was a long night. The 350th Artillery shelled an eleven-acre spot of woods with 9,000 Germans in it the night before we were ordered to take Metz," he said. "There was not a tree standing in the morning, or a German in sight. We could see the city of Metz from our positions. But five minutes before we were to move out at 5:00 a.m. Captain Bison called out 'Hold it!' That was when a messenger on a motorcycle arrived at the scene. The rider was elated; he told them the glad news. He said, 'We had some hard times in those trenches and we were plenty ready to go home. There was no good time in this war, but at last this part was over!' "

There were a number of individual citations for bravery, and one entire battalion belonging to the 367th Infantry was awarded the Croix de Guerre. On the morning of the signing of the armistice the 365th Infantry had taken several hundred yards of the battle front, the 366th had captured and was still in possession of several kilometers of territory, and the 367th was nearest to the coveted stronghold of Metz of any of the units of the Allied Armies.[36] It was here that the 1st Battalion distinguished itself by coming to the rescue of the 56th Infantry on the left. Captain Morris and Lieutenants Hunton, Dabney, and Davidson were instrumental in having the terrific fire which was being directed at the regiment, turned onto their own organization, thus enabling the suffering troops to retire to safety; they were at the same time able to hold their own ground and take over the territory of the retiring soldiers. For this action the battalion was cited in glowing terms by a French general, and awarded the Croix de Guerre. It was also given special mention by Major General Ballou.[37]

Before the armistice that ended the war was signed, the 92nd Division casualties totaled 3,534. The division could list Oise-Aisne, St. Mihiel, and the Meuse Argonne campaign to its honors. No amount of publicity today will make up for the publicity these soldiers did not get after the war for their deeds.

On December 15, 1918, the 92nd Division moved to Mayenns, the American embarkation center. On January 30, 1919, the division started moving to Breast and its leading elements started home. The last elements arrived in New York on March 6, 1919, and the 367th Infantry was sent to Camp Meade, Maryland, where it was demobilized on March 7, 1919.

3

Lest We Forget

T he Dutch liner *Rotterdam* arrived at American shores Monday, February 17, 1919, from France with 4,367 troops on board, and was berthed in Hoboken and Jersey City. Among the men on the *Rotterdam* were the field and staff headquarters company of the medical detachment and companies G, I, K, L, and M of the 367th Infantry, New York's Negro draft regiment. The men had been trained at Yaphank under Col. James A. Moss and were known in the army as Moss's Buffaloes.

The voyage across waters that resembled massive walls of waves was a great endurance for all of them. Many men received life-threatening injuries on the way home. When they finally arrived, a good number were convalescents.

The regiment was cited by General Pershing. The Negro soldiers had proved themselves fine assault troops. Their casualties were about ten percent. There were fifty-one officers and 1,484 enlisted men of the 367th Regiment on the *Rotterdam*.

Among the senior officers on the *Rotterdam* were Brig. Gen. Joseph B. Irwin of the Sixth Division, Brig. Gen. Edward Burr, in command of the 117th Field Artillery Brigade, which

Above: *New York's famous 369th (old 15th) Infantry arrive from France at Hoboken, NJ, 1919.*

Below: *351st Field Artillery (part of Squadron "A"), on the deck of the* Louisville *February 17, 1919.*

was attacking in front of Metz when the armistice was signed, and Lt. Col. R. H. Dunlap, the only marine officer in France who commanded a field artillery brigade. One of the wounded officers on board was Capt. A. J. O'Keefe of Fort Leavenworth, Kansas, of the 18th Infantry, First Division. He would wear the Legion of Honor Cross.[38]

New York was outstanding for the fine treatment of its black veterans. The 369th returned to the city on February 12, 1919, and marched in a victory parade up Fifth Avenue a few days later. The first New York soldiers to come home, Colonel Hayward's troops, marched in the impressively solid French phalanx formation to the music of Jim Europe's band, which on its own brought out many spectators who hoped for some good jazz. But in Europe they had marched to only French marches, and so with a steady stride they stepped, and from under their battered tin hats, eyes that had looked straight at death were kept to the front.[39]

The parade route included Twenty-third Street and Fifth Avenue to 145th Street and Lenox Avenue. The men were proud of themselves and their organization. Their rows of bayonets glanced in the sun. The Germans had given them the title of the *"Bludurstig schwarze manner,"* or "Bloodthirsty black men." Most of them were grim-visaged from force of habit, and the helmet chin straps added a hardening touch, so New York got a pretty fair idea of how they had impressed the Germans.

Lt. James Europe, in spite of reports that he was down with pneumonia, was at the head of his celebrated band whose "jazz" was in demand among American soldiers in all parts of France. They had little breath left, but made a brave effort when they finally got into their own community. Five of the instruments in the band were kettle drums, presented by the French as a mark of the esteem in which the regiment was held by its French comrades.

When Colonel Hayward reached a point opposite the grandstand in Harlem, John J. Lyons presented him with a resolution written by Nicholas Murray Butler, on behalf of residents of Harlem, saying:

Above: *The "Buffaloes," 367th Infantry Regiment, singing the National Anthem in front of the Union League Club, New York, 1918.*

Below: *Parade in New York City in honor of soldiers returning from France, 1919.*

The residents of Harlem from which the 369th Infantry was so largely recruited wish to give a special and hearty greeting to Colonel Hayward and the officers and men of the old Fighting 15th who have made so fine a record for patriotism and courage on the soil of France.

No American soldiers saw harder or more constant fighting and none gave a better account of themselves, whether in the Champagne, at Chateau Thierry, at the Saint Mihiel salient, or in the Argonne. When fighting was to be done this regiment was there. Two Governments have given this regiment special citations for bravery in action, and among the officers and men are many who have won for themselves exceptional distinction in the service of their country.[40]

After the parade, city officials entertained the troops with a dinner in the armory of the 71st New York Infantry. It was the first and only time in its service that the whole regiment was assembled under one roof.

Recreational center opened by black women for soldiers, Newark, NJ, 1919.

On the way to Camp Travis in San Antonio, after arriving at Camp Bowie, Fort Worth, Walter Potts had an experience that he would never forget. He had been at Fort Worth for about an hour when someone yelled out his name: "Corporal Potts, Corporal Potts, come to the front." He could not imagine why they were calling him. He said, "I rushed myself along to get up." Then they told him that there was a woman from Denison who had come to see him. Of course, all of the guys wanted to know what was going on. They always said that he was a ladies' man. The woman was Willie Brooks, a friend of the family. Willie had just stopped by to see if he was in the group of soldiers so she could relay the news of his arrival to his family. She was so happy to see him that she started to cry. The head of the family that Willie was employed by had also been stationed in France. His family had been notified and his arrival back home was scheduled for him to return via Fort Worth. There had been no previous mention of any black soldiers returning to Fort Worth.

Walter brought with him from France one of the bravest records achieved by anyone in the war. He earned campaign streamers, medals, and other battle honors in recognition for valorous deeds. (Despite the efforts of the personnel at the French Embassy, the records of the French Army were not made available to the author.) The bolo knife mounted on the wall in the living room of Walter's home exhibited a very eerie elegance. It served as a reminder of the war, but it also gave a tangible piece of evidence of the crudeness of the weapons that were used.

The awards and citations that the men of the 92nd received were numerous. The entire first battalion of the 367th Infantry was cited for bravery in its participation in the drive toward Metz and was awarded the Croix de Guerre, while the colors of the regiment were decorated by order of the French high command.[41]

One of the most sensational feats involving the bolo knife in the war was performed by two privates, Henry Johnson of Albany, New York, and Needham Roberts of Trenton, New Jersey, both members of the 369th Infantry. While the men were on guard at a small outpost in May 1918, a strong raiding

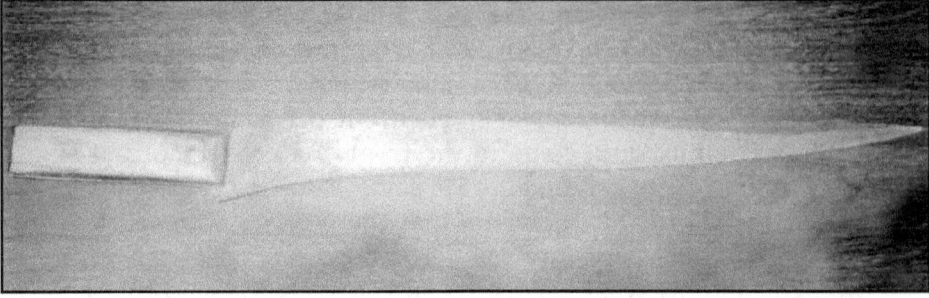

Bolo knife.

party of Germans numbering almost twenty made a surprise attack, wounding the two Negroes. When the Germans were within fighting distance, Johnson opened fire, and Roberts, lying on the ground, threw grenades. The Germans continued to advance, and as the two black men were about to be captured, Johnson drew his bolo knife from his belt and attacked the Germans in a hand-to-hand encounter. He succeeded in freeing Roberts from the Germans who were dragging him away, and he slashed several so mercilessly that they died of their wounds. The killing of at least four of the enemy and the wounding of perhaps twice as many more caused this encounter to become known as "The Battle of Henry Johnson." Both men received the Croix de Guerre for their gallantry.[42]

Walter remembered an incident that he was not proud of. He said, "It was a time when it was either 'me or them'." One day around noon the men in the unit were making preparations for assigning men to guard the area for the night watch. Suddenly, they heard a rustle in a nearby bush. Almost instantly, Walter fired the Springfield rifle that had become a part of his daily dress. The intruder had been killed instantly. One German soldier lay dead, but there had been two soldiers hiding in the bushes. When the other German soldier ran, Walter fired the Springfield again and stopped the running target with a single shot. Later, two more German soldiers came to see what had happened to their comrades. These next two soldiers did not come in close enough to the camp to be within firing range. They did, however, relay the tragic news to their command, and later that night the 367th was attacked with a renewed vengeance. Fourteen men lost their lives when they decided to take cover in the bushes. Walter and the rest of the men dug trenches and fought the Germans for two solid hours, firing their weapons as fast as they could load them. When the Germans quit firing, the night was still and quiet.

The one-pound shell that was placed on the piano in the living room of Walter's home was yet another reminder of how raw the weapons of war were. Walter wanted to keep this shell because one that had been fired very near had almost taken his life when he was in the combat zone.

The shell had hit their camp and destroyed everything in the surrounding area. Walter went to the captain and asked if he could have one of the live shells, since one had almost taken him out. The captain said, "It's dangerous, but if you can disarm it you can have it." With skilled and careful hands Walter took the one-pound shell apart and poured the powder out. He then put the top back on it. Handing the empty shell to the captain, he asked that he take the top off of the harmless shell. The captain was astonished that the shell was empty. He told Walter that he had never seen that done. In a very serious tone of voice he also told him that the task was too dangerous for anyone to perform. Walter responded, "Not if you know how." The captain said, "I told you that if you could disarm it you could have it. You can have it; you deserve it." Then as an afterthought the captain asked, "What did you do with the powder that was inside?" Walter told him that he had dug a hole and buried the powder in it. If the powder lay on top of the ground and was somehow ignited, anyone nearby would be blown to pieces. The shell certainly earned its place on the piano.

When Walter returned home, there was a parade for the Negro soldiers that lived in the area. The people in the town of Bonham were astonished at the hundreds who came from many miles away. All who turned out to see them, especially the residents, were mighty impressed by the magnificent appearance of these fighting men who were a part of a regiment that had been cited for bravery. The men marched proudly with the natural precision of soldiers who had long ago mas-

World War I U.S. Army discharge.

tered the technique of their profession. The communities greet-
ed their own boys for blocks along the streets of Bonham. The
sidewalks were packed, the windows were filled with faces,
and the roofs held more. Hundreds of flags fluttered—American flags, service flags, and "Welcome Home" banners. When
the soldiers finally arrived in their own part of town, the crowd

went wild with joy. Each person in the throng seemed to be shouting to a particular soldier and begging for a glance of recognition. The unison of voices became a mighty roar.

For more than one hundred years, the Buffalo Soldiers' role in the settlement of the American West has been virtually invisible in the historical accounts of the period. Their heroic efforts have been rewarded philatelically by the U.S. Postal Service with the issuance of a 29-cent commemorative stamp. The stamp is dedicated to their triumph and pride despite their hardships.

Gen. Colin Powell, former chairman of the Joint Chiefs of Staff, worked on a project to see that an old debt of recognition was finally paid. After more than ten years of work, Powell increased public awareness when he dedicated a magnificent memorial to the Buffalo Soldiers of all wars. The monument includes a bronze sculpture of an equestrian Buffalo Soldier with a natural pond behind him and a reflecting pool in front of him. Thousands made the trip to hear the dedication at Fort Leavenworth, Kansas. On July 27, 1992, a group of men no one really knew was honored to meet with some of the due recognition and reward the former soldiers have begun to receive. Some of them achieved historical importance more than one hundred years ago. Their stories are finally being told via a program that explains the history of the soldiers.

Numerous articles in the *Denison Herald* document how honored Walter's family felt to be able to pay tribute to him. His ninety-eighth birthday was especially touching, for he received an autographed poster of the Buffalo Solider Monument statue from Cmdr. Carlton G. Philpot, chairman of the Buffalo Soldier Monument Committee. Commander Philpot not only wished that he have a happy birthday, but also stated that Walter was the oldest documented Buffalo Soldier.

An autographed photograph of Walter Potts and some pictures of his unit are displayed in an exhibit at the Wadsworth Atheneum. The museum is America's oldest public art museum, in Hartford, Connecticut. It houses the Amistad Foundation's African American Collection. Some of his medals were also included in the special exhibit to honor African Americans in the United States military. His photograph has been fea-

Above: *Buffalo Soldier Monument poster.*

Below: *Veterans of World War I 75th Anniversary Honor.*

The Veterans of World War I
in Observance of the 1-Year Celebration:
"A Grateful Nation DOES Remember"
the 75th Anniversary of the "War To End All Wars,"
acknowledges and sincerely appreciates

Walter Edward Potts, Sr.

to our special appeal for
the continuation of VWWI and its programs.

Leonard D. Corbin
National Commander

Dana J. Pyle
National QM-Adjutant

tured in the Willard Scott birthday honor segment of NBC's *Today* show. A member of his former unit commended the articles that were published in *The Torch*, a newspaper that honors the veterans of World War I. *The Torch* has also recognized Walter Potts, the author's grandfather, as the oldest World War I veteran.

4

Childhood Roots

Walter E. Potts was born January 9, 1892, in Denison, Texas, the son of William and Mollie Potts. A happy household in those early years in Denison is how he recalled his childhood.

William's father, Joe Burton, was from a small community located north of Muskogee, Oklahoma. Joe was born into slavery. The exact date of Joe's birth is unknown. William listed North Carolina as the state of birth for both of his parents on the 1900 census records. No one knows what Joe Burton's real African name was (Joe Burton was a slave name). Walter smiled as he shared a bit of information that his father shared with him: "Joe Burton was from the Indian country." William's mother was Henrietta. Her maiden name is unknown. As was the situation with many other slave families, her home was divided. Some families endured painful separations and from time to time they were never reunited with the entire family. Joe and Henrietta made a simple yet comfortable home and prepared a place for their family.

Walter was very proud of his heritage. He remembered the

town that was named after the Potts family. He told how he became a part of the family. "During slavery time," he said, "blacks were not free men. Negroes were the property of the white man. Wherever you went you had to go under the white man's name." Potts needed some slaves for his plantation. He traveled to Oklahoma, where he purchased Joe Burton from a slave owner near Muskogee." Joe had a young son who became very upset that his father was about to be sold and separated from him. It is understandable that the boy wanted very much to come with his father. Walter chuckled about the story William later told. He said the young boy kept crying and saying over and over again, "I want to come with my daddy, I want to come with my daddy." Potts finally agreed to let the boy go also, and so he got another slave for free. Potts brought Joe Burton and his young son to the Potts plantation.

Pottsboro is a community about six miles west of Denison. Although Pottsboro was founded as a railroad town in 1878, its roots extend back before the Civil War. Long before any white people settled in that part of North Texas, plains and prairie Indians hunted in the area, especially the Caddo and Wichita tribes. In 1838 the Republic of Texas authorized the survey and construction of a national road from Austin to the Red River. To guard the road, a military post was established in 1840. A small community called Georgetown developed near the fort.

William Potts was born in July 1865. He grew up in the Pottsboro and Denison areas. He developed into a robust, hard-working man. When he was ready to be married he proposed to a beautiful young woman from Ravenna, Mollie Oliphant. Her parents were Fountain Oliphant and Patsy Espey. Both of Mollie's parents were from Menden, Louisiana. The couple appreciated the protection of real estate ownership and managed a flourishing farm for many years.

William and Mollie Potts had their first child, Lu Berta, in April 1889. Walter Edward was their second child, born in 1892. Their third child, James Roscoe, was born in May 1900. Lu Berta helped her mother with the rearing of young Walter since she was almost three years old when he was born. She had the responsibility of caring for him, and later she had to care for her mother. More than eight years passed before James Roscoe was born. Mollie had given birth to two other children during those years. Recorded in the census for 1900 it is indicated that she is the mother of five children. The number of children living is stated to be three; William and Mollie had lost two of their precious children.

Walter remembered well the regional smallpox plagues early in the twentieth century that ravaged the Denison area. The lives of his mother and sister were claimed. Mollie and Lu Berta perished in the plague that occurred around 1902. Lu Berta was twelve years old when she died.

Devastated by the losses, William was left with two youthful boys and no home in which to rear them. The bereavement period for him was a long one. Many people died in the plague as it continued for months. It is believed that William probably suffered from depression as well. The pain stayed fresh in his mind. His sorrow was so great that it threatened to overwhelm him. Despite the efforts he made to adjust himself to the loss of his loved ones, nothing worked. He chose to be deeply engaged in his work.

Eventually, he made the necessary arrangements to change the environment in which he had experienced so much grief. For the last time, he left the home that was located at 410 Walker Street. The place that he once shared with his loving wife, daughter, and two young sons no longer held the promise of prosperity. (Some twenty years later, young Walter would return to Walker Street as a man and share a home with his wife and family.)

In due time William went back to his job as a porter with the railroad. Porters were expected to follow a rigid code of behavior. William was willing to put up with it because the job brought a certain amount of status. Porters were highly respected in their communities. Diligently and graciously, he assisted passengers with their baggage, tended the sleeping berths, cleaned ashtrays and spittoons, and shined shoes. The pain that William felt inside could not be openly expressed, as he had to be cheerful when executing all of the orders. Consideration of the passengers was of prime importance. Employment requirements were that he travel back and forth on the train routes to Denver, Colorado. William had to make arrangements for the two small boys that were the only surviving members left of his immediate family. Consequently, the boys went to live with their grandparents. The bonds that were made and the years of teaching his boys had received from Mollie's family would not be overlooked.

William came back often to visit the boys. Time permitting, he would also visit many people in the surrounding communities to tell stories of his adventures on the trains. He would often openly express the pain as well as the joy that he felt when he came to see the boys at the Oliphant farm. He would bring little things of various sorts from the cities that he visited.

Sometimes during their conversations, questions would arise which he could not answer. Every now and then the boys would ask if they could go home to live with him in the city. They longed to see the big cities. They also yearned for the chance to experience some of the exciting adventures that they could only dream about. William did his best to answer them. Using his best judgment when these situations came up, he made a favorable and lasting impression on them.

The boys never went to live with their father. When William did visit, the family always spent quality time together. Walter remembered that his father was there for every holiday that he could make. They were so proud of him and tremendously happy that he could come home. Walter and James Roscoe looked forward to receiving the clothes and toys that their father would bring to them.

Over the years the boys had grown so attached and devoted to the older folks that there was nothing that could take them away from their home on the farm. In his later years William suffered a crippling illness that developed into paralysis. He was confined to a wheelchair the last four painful years of his life.

Walter was nine years old when Mollie's father, Fountain Oliphant, took him and his brother James Roscoe to his home in Ravenna. Shared grief drew the families even closer together. The comfort and joy that they shared would make a special bond which would last a lifetime. Suffering the losses of the smallpox plague was a great blow to almost everyone in the community. Walter spent the remainder of his childhood in Ravenna, in the home of his grandparents. He remembered that James Roscoe was "just a baby" when they moved to the Oliphant home. Walter and James Roscoe grew up together for a while there. The boys were taught the precise operations of a farm. The attention, kindness, and affection that were given to them by their grandparents made a positive impact on their lives.

When James Roscoe became ill, suffering from an extremely high fever, severe headaches, and diarrhea, his grandparents feared the worst. Despite the efforts of the doctors and the midwives, James Roscoe died of typhoid fever at the tender age of fourteen. Walter would wonder for years to come why he was still healthy. He would again attend a funeral and bury a beloved family member.

Walter left school after completing only the third grade. He would become a skilled farmer, carpenter, and blacksmith. Also, he was successful at performing the many tasks that were necessary to run a farm. His grandparents' attention to him now was not limited to the responsibility of caring for the only child that was left in that family. There was also the fear that he may succumb to one of the many illnesses that had claimed the lives of all but his father. Their comfort was his support throughout his life. They taught him valuable lessons that would benefit him in life.

Walter worked all of his life. Although he had to leave school after the third grade, he could already read and write by the time he had to quit school. He said they taught a lot of practical things in school during those days. The knowledge that students gained by the time they finished the third grade was probably equivalent to high school by today's standards.

The first school for African American students in the rural communities of Ravenna and Mulberry was called Mulberry School Number 92. School records have been destroyed, but it is well known that the school was inadequate. The school did exist, however, and produced some great citizens. The students were educated by dedicated, brave teachers and therefore should be remembered. Mulberry School Number 92 is

believed to have been established in the 1880s. In the beginning the school classes were held in the local church building.
It was staffed by very few teachers.

Ravenna is a small rural community that is located in
northwestern Fannin County. The community was settled
about 1875. It was named Ravenna because of the great number of ravines in and around the area. Mulberry is the next
nearest community to Ravenna. Ravenna had a population of
237 in 1890, 415 in 1920, and 248 in 1940. Ravenna now
has a population of 186.

5

The Many Fortunes
of Life

With a quick smile and ready laugh, Walter could relate story after story about his marriage to Eva Brown of Honey Grove. They were married on May 22, 1919. Eva endured the long wait for his return home from the war in France. The couple was married within a scant two months after his discharge from the army.

Numerous industrial opportunities became available to women when workers were needed to replace men drafted into military service. More than 20,000 black women left their homes and domestic jobs during the period of December 1, 1918, to June 30, 1919. Eva realized the worth of educating the children of their tiny community, and therefore continued to teach at the small school.

Walter and Eva owned their first home on Walker Street in Denison. Some twenty years earlier, William and Mollie Potts had begun to raise their young family at their home on Walker Street. Walter had strong feelings about the family that was taken from him at such an early age. Although he did not always openly express his feelings about it, he was in tune with

Walter E. Potts,
1974.

the past of the area, and chose to remain there all of his life—even during the mass migration of blacks from the South during and after World War I.

Millions were leaving the South to escape segregation and discrimination. African American journalist Robert Sengstacke Abbott founded the *Chicago Defender* in 1905. Abbott's editorial creed was to fight against disfranchisement. He advertised Chicago so effectively that even migrants heading for northern cities sought information and assistance from the pages of the newspaper. *The Crisis,* a publication sponsored by the NAACP and edited by W. E. B. Dubois, came out in 1910. *The Defender* and *The Crisis* reached national prominence during the mass exodus. The Potts family sought the strength of each other and valued the stability of those who had come before them. They decided to stay and make Denison their home. Their wise decisions regarding business and real estate transactions were essential to establishing a secure and financially independent future for themselves and their families.

Walter met Sam Rayburn during his first campaign for public office, and boasted about a "great friendship" with the late House Speaker. He did a lot of local campaigning in Fannin County on behalf of Rayburn. During the time Rayburn served as representative of Fannin County, he would often go down to Mulberry and visit with Walter and discuss local issues. Rayburn was concerned about the opinions of the local black community, and Walter was the spokesperson. He said, "Why, Mr. Sam thought he couldn't do without me. I was out by daylight and burned midnight oil getting votes for him, a good man, a man I loved." "Mister Sam" is how Walter and numerous others referred to Sam Rayburn. Sam Rayburn was one of America's most powerful and influential politicians. He was a member of the U.S. House of Representatives from 1913 to 1961. He also served as Speaker of the House of Representatives for all but four years between 1940 and 1961—longer than any other in American history.

In 1907 racial segregation, practiced in Texas as throughout the South, was an issue only in that the moderates (including Rayburn) constantly battled the radicals to prevent them from coming down even harder on blacks. Segregation was an accepted way of life; Rayburn never questioned it. It was seldom mentioned in campaigns, but the issue was always like a time bomb.[43]

After each congressional session, Rayburn headed to Bonham, where in 1916 he had built a home. It was there that he was happiest, mingling with his constituents and welcoming friends.

One of the many self-taught skills that Walter Potts possessed was carpentry. He was proud to have been consulted and hired by Rayburn to be one of the chief carpenters when the fourteen-room house that served as his home was built. Although Rayburn's relationship with Walter was entirely political, Rayburn always seemed to temper power with humil-

ity to establish himself as one of the most beloved political fig-
ures in the black community.

After 1948, he continued resisting federal intervention in
racial matters, but he began in small ways prodding the South
to lead in solving its own problems. In Texas, he urged Attorney General Price Daniel and members of the legislature to
abolish the state poll tax, which had effectively disfranchised
blacks and other minorities for generations. Only seven states
still retained the much despised tax. He warned other southerners that federal intervention was inevitable if blacks continued to be denied basic rights. "You can't filibuster forever,"
he told them.[44]

Although the Civil Rights Act of 1957 was far less com-
prehensive than that of 1964, strategy evolved to enable the
earlier act to pass gave advocates invaluable experience in getting the second bill through. Any voting rights bill had to be
designed so as to reduce the possibility of a Senate filibuster
that would kill it. The attitude of Speaker Sam Rayburn would
be important if this trip were to be avoided—not so much because of his influence in the House itself but because of his
prestige and influence among Southerners in both the House
and Senate.[45]

In January 1956, Congressman Richard Bolling of Mis-
souri approached Rayburn about supporting a voting rights
bill, aimed primarily at disfranchised southern blacks. The
need for such legislation had been discussed among liberals in
and out of Congress for years, and now the time seemed ripe.
The Eisenhower administration, through the office of Attorney
General Herbert Brownell, was examining growing complaints
of civil rights denial and trying to decide whether to propose
its own rights bill in 1956, a presidential election year.

Bolling, one of Rayburn's young lieutenants and self-ap-
pointed liaison between the House leadership and the liberal
House Democratic Study Group, decided that if any civil
rights legislation was to get through Congress, the Speaker's
full support was essential. He was needed, Bolling noted later,
"not so much because of his influence in the House itself but
because of his prestige and influence among Southerners in
both the House and Senate."

Bolling, as the liberals' chief strategist, decided that the best course was deliberately to impede the bill's progress even more, so that it reached the House floor before adjournment but too late to be taken up by the Senate. House liberals would have a civil rights vote on which to campaign in the fall. Bolling discussed that tactic with Rayburn, advising the Speaker to inform Lyndon B. Johnson that the Senate was getting only temporary relief. The House would certainly pass and send to the Senate a new civil rights bill early in 1957. "I understand what you are saying," Rayburn replied impatiently.

Although he tried, Rules Committee Chairman Howard Smith this time could not block a civil rights bill. The momentum was too strong, even for the much-feared conservative coalition. On July 16 the measure reached the House floor. Opponents sought to expedite the debate. With a quick vote, they hoped to catch the liberals, notorious for their absences, unprepared. Rayburn saw through this strategy at once. He found Bolling in the corridor and told him sharply: "You'd better get your boys here quickly." Rayburn never explained how he could sense trouble brewing on the House floor, but he had that ability, as scores of members have testified over the years.[46]

Bolling took Rayburn's warning as a good sign. "I knew then for the first time," he said later, "that I had been correct in believing that Rayburn would be a supporter of the civil rights bill."

What Bolling did not know was that even before his first meeting with Rayburn early in 1956, the Texan had been reappraising his views on civil rights. He supported a voting rights bill, not only because it made sense politically, but, more importantly, he felt it was right for the nation. He had agonized over the whole question of racial equality and segregation for years, especially since the Supreme Court put the issue squarely before the nation with its landmark school desegregation decision, *Brown vs. The Board of Education of Topeka, Kansas.* "If you had been on that Court," Rayburn said shortly after the 1954 ruling, "you'd have voted exactly as they voted if you were an honest man."

On the record, Rayburn was no champion of civil rights before 1956. He had helped block Truman's Fair Employment

Practices Commission bill, had consistently opposed federal anti-poll tax and anti-lynch legislation (although he supported state action on these issues), and, in the heat of his own campaigns, had stood firmly for preserving racial segregation. But times were changing, and he sensed the need for a new outlook, in himself and in the nation. "Men are not angels," he told the graduating class of Syracuse University in June. "It is not, therefore, criminal that inequities should exist among us. But it would be criminal if we should ignore them. This we will not do."[47]

Politically, Rayburn was walking a fine line. His national responsibilities and his conscience lay on one side; his role as representative of a strongly prosegregation constituency on the other. But he always believed that if he was thinking straight, he could fly in the face of public opinion at home, that he could go home and convince his people that he was right. He despised colleagues who were, as he put it, "afraid of their districts."

On one occasion Rayburn faced a minor problem that well indicates how he handled racial issues. During the 1950s he received a request for an appointment with a visiting delegation of schoolchildren from the district. A staff member pointed out that the children were black and asked Rayburn if he would see them. Rayburn unhesitatingly agreed. No public display was made of his friendliness toward the black children, however. No reporters were told of the visit, and contrary to his frequent practice, he lunched with the children in the privacy of his office rather than taking them to a more visible dining area.[48]

Frequently intervening to break committee deadlocks, Rayburn embroiled himself more deeply in drafting and enacting specific bills than he had in years. In 1960 he went to bat for a new civil rights bill, a Democratic priority, lending his support to a discharge petition that would force its release by the rules committee. It was leadership the times demanded, but it was risky.[49]

Walter Potts said that in 1961, when Sam Rayburn died, he was one of the first to be called. He was expected to be there. "Mr. Sam was a blessing," he said. The political giant's aid and moral commitment during his political career would always be remembered. The house in Bonham today has been restored to its 1961 condition. It is an elegant structure that reflects the style of Rayburn, who lived a comfortable yet modest lifestyle.

Walter was an unofficial member of the Fannin County School Board. He was the individual most responsible for the development of communication between the school board and the black community. One of his goals was to have one of the first schools brought to Ravenna and Mulberry. The first frame structure was a one-room building. Many improvements were needed.

For many years Walter was a spokesperson for the community. He did not miss an opportunity to tell the people what to do, and how to become organized in order to get what was needed. Walter had a decided influence on people, an effect that made many people feel that their lives had been changed, deepened, and enriched. The position of school board trustee afforded Walter the opportunity to be the only black representative on the committee with seven other white males. The job was voluntary, but Walter did not mind that.

He remembered the night that he received the news of the proposal to donate the old Mulberry school to the blacks. When the proposal was made, he said, "Now you've done the wrong thing. You're in for a surprise at the meeting on Wednesday night." When he attended the meeting, Walter demanded that a regular school building be built so the children would not have to continue to attend school in the church building. Although the committee was receptive to the idea, instead of building a new school the officials requested that they use the old Mulberry school building that was once occupied by the white school students. Not only that, the residents of the community had to raise the money to have the old building moved from the present location across town. That same evening, Walter called a community meeting, and agreements were made to pay for the movement of the school building. It would cost $50, and the money was to be raised by contributions. Walter received the money, the building was moved, and he quickly started to formulate other ways to help in this education effort. The School Board Committee was receptive to the ideas for suggested improvements to be made to the school.

Walter also worked on the Katy Railroad for a number of years. As a handyman he mastered repairing appliances that contained electrical wires, and made all types of furniture. While working for the railroad, on his off day, usually Thursday, he would pick up furniture, radios, and television sets from people who lived in town and in the surrounding communities. Using his truck he made the house calls as a handyman, as people were always in need of having items repaired. Many times they simply threw things out. From time to time Walter would repair a discarded item and resell it, making a nice profit. He acquired a number of items during this time. One oak table that he was especially proud of had a beautifully detailed hand carving of the first Roman Catholic church under glass. Another treasured item was a hand-held saw that he made from scratch.

Walter helped build the Houston Street Katy overpass in Denison. Sometimes he had to cross the Red River on a ferry to cut bois d'arc posts for highline wires.

The many accomplishments throughout his career continued as an odyssey of personal discovery. He proudly stated, "You have to have a dream—I had a dream. I made it!"

Walter Edward Potts had three little words to live by that would make this a better world for all mankind: "Thou Shalt Not." He believed that if these words from the heart of the Bible were taken to heart there would be no problems, no wars. A profoundly religious man, he quoted from the Bible, "Keep my commandments and everything will go well with you all your days." But alas, he knew men were still disobedient, still doing the same "ole thing," still fighting. Walter joined the church and was baptized at an early age. He was an energetic member for many years at Hopewell Church. In later years he attended Haven Chapel United Methodist Church with his daughter. He said regardless where he ended up, his faith would stay the same. "I love the Lord. I have been obedient to God's ways all of my life." He gave recognition to the Lord for his longevity.

Walter planted a garden every year, loved to visit and go

to church. The garden became truly a sight to behold, with tomatoes, mustard greens, onions, and an assortment of herbs used as fresh garnishing for the delicious meals that his daughter Violet June cooked. Old tools overflowed from the backyard shed that housed some of the remnants of the old farming equipment.

To relax, he liked to sit on the spacious front porch of his home that he shared with Violet. The most comfortable place for him was on the banister. Walter said, "I sit here to rest my back." Occasionally, he would prop one foot up on a stool and still maintain a graceful correct posture. His reflexes stayed excellently sharp as he swiftly swatted a fly that landed on his

*Eva Potts
(date
unknown).*

forehead, then immediately waved to some people driving by the house. The breeze billowed through the many trees that surround the property. The lush green lawn added to the beauty of the setting.

He laughed and said, "I'll see you next year about this time. I already have a good start on 106 with a lot of memories behind me and a lot of living ahead of me. I live each day for that day and let tomorrow take care of itself. You know tomorrow may never come."

Walter and Eva enjoyed a marriage that continued for more than forty years. Their forty-first anniversary was spent with Eva in the hospital, where she had struggled with an illness for more than six months. She died June 1, 1960, from complications resulting from that long illness. Walter made a beautiful little birdhouse to go in the tree that he planted at her gravesite. The tree would provide shade from the sun and shelter from the sometimes harsh weather. The charming birdhouse ensured constant life and endless songs at the location. All through the years, Walter made sure the blue paint was kept fresh.

Eva had been born December 24, 1892. She was soft-spoken and had a gentle personality. Her dark brunette hair matched her eyes. Eva was inspired by her father and earned a living by becoming a teacher. She graduated from Wiley College in Marshall. She taught at the only school for African American students in the rural community of Ravenna. The school served as a church and a community center. Long before Eva received an official teacher's certificate in 1918, many youngsters in the community benefited from her knowledge. She was good with them and very patient.

Eva's parents were E. E. and Violet Brown. E. E. was called "Father Brown" by almost everyone. He was a minister and an educator. Father Brown and Violet were from Louisiana. He had attended college in Louisiana, obtained teaching credentials, and was a teacher there. Walter remembered seeing the credentials: "Father Brown had a Louisiana Certificate that says 'he was who he said he was.' He brought the first program (educational) to our community."

Father Brown fought for freedom rights for blacks in the

South. The fight became overwhelming as he braved the dangerous professions of teaching and religion in his quest to achieve his primary goal. Father Brown was either in an unassailable position or recklessly courageous. At the time it was believed that blacks were likely to imbibe seditious and incendiary doctrines through their reading. Laws were passed to ensure that the blacks would not be educated. A surprisingly large number of them nevertheless learned at least the fundamentals. Rather than face mounting violence and legal restrictions, the Brown family decided to become a part of the migration from Louisana. The repressive climate of racial violence and segregation led many black families to pour out of the area. They left to escape sharecropping, worsening economic conditions, and the increasing number of lynch mobs. They sought higher wages, better homes, and political rights.

Migration from the South has long been a significant feature of black history. The early exodus from the South occurred between 1879 and 1881, when about 60,000 African Americans moved into Kansas, while others settled in the Oklahoma Indian Territories in search of social and economic freedom.

Benjamin "Pap" Singleton (1809-1892), a former slave born in Nashville, Tennessee, was the leader of the "Exoduster Movement" of 1879. In later years he was accorded the title "Father of the Exodus." In the late 1860s, Singleton and his associates urged blacks to acquire farmland in Tennessee, but whites would not sell productive land to them. As an alternative, Singleton began scouting land in Kansas. Yellow fever ravaged many river towns at the time of the Exodus to Kansas. Because many of the migrants who stopped over in these towns were sick, unwashed, and poverty stricken, it was assumed by city officials that they must be potential disease carriers. This caused great alarm in cities that imposed unnecessary quarantine measures to discourage future migrants.

The Brown family decided to settle in Honey Grove, Texas, when they left Louisiana. Honey Grove owes its name to David Crockett. In December 1835, Crockett and his company of volunteers from Tennessee were en route to San Antonio, where they gave their lives for Texas Independence.

They made camp in a grove of trees just north of the present public square. Here Crockett found a flowing spring and many trees containing honey. The letter from Crockett from San Augustine on January 9, 1836, to his family in Tennessee gave a description of a place he called "the honey grove." He said it was the garden spot of the world.

Eva had one sister, Isceola, and one brother, Waler. Isceola was born February 22, 1889. She grew up to follow in her father's footsteps in the education of the people. Eva enlarged the family commitment to education when she also became a teacher. Isceola was remarkably effective as a teacher, and after her retirement she realized that there was still work to be done in the community. The blacks in the city of Honey Grove lacked an adult education program. Isceola negotiated with the Fannin County School Board and decided to come out of retirement. She was responsible for the organization of the first adult education program for the city. She also taught many of the classes. Isceloa lived to be almost 100 years old. She died on April 13, 1988. The city of Honey Grove recognizes the commitment of all of the early African American pioneers each year in September.

No one is certain of the original family name that Mother Violet Brown was a part of. As was the situation with many other slave families, her home was divided. Many times family members were never reunited. When Walter remembered her, he said, "All of the people that knew her knew that she was loyal to the people." Along with Father Brown she now had a family that could remain together. Theirs was a family that was rare during that time. To be able to teach the people in the community was an honor that was cherished. This honor often had to be kept secret, or one could face sudden death for simply teaching black children to read or write.

Father Brown was a symbol of the unintimidated and articulated, strong black man. Mother Violet was a powerful woman who had a very positive influence on Eva and her siblings. She was also on a mission to help the people. As much as she knew that this help stirred and divided the town, she knew it was the right thing to do. These early struggles and sacrifices helped to mould Walter the man. Father Brown was so committed to the education of the people that he defied the secrecy. He journeyed in search of a safe place with the hope of finding greater opportunities and better treatment, where he could teach the children in peace. He thought he had found the perfect location when he crossed the Red River and went to Oklahoma with the plans to build a new school. The relocation was not the haven that he had hoped for.

Father Brown fell victim to the white supremacy that he had fled. Since he was known as a gifted leader, the Ku Klux Klan searched for him. Local efforts to suppress the outlaw organizations were on the whole unsuccessful. The Ku Klux Klan, an organization formed in 1866 to intimidate blacks and other ethnic and religious minorities, was the first of many secret terrorist organizations. They were organized in the South for the purpose of reestablishing white authority. When the Klan finally found Father Brown, he was brutally murdered. The murder was committed to scare other blacks.

The school building had just been completed. A new school, modest that it was, would have clearly benefited not only the children but all of the people. It was destroyed and then later burned. Father Brown was a hero in that he offered the educational experience as well as the religious experience for people that would have otherwise not known these things. The first free Negro school in Fannin County was not legally authorized until January 4, 1881. Father Brown and Mother Violet are buried in Honey Grove.

Walter and Eva Potts had three children: Walter Jr., G. B. of Waller, and Violet Garrett of Denison. Violet June was the first child for Walter and Eva. She was a beautiful and healthy daughter born on March 28, 1921. Violet June had a very close relationship with her mother. She took great pride in being named for her grandmother. She was destined to grow up to follow in the footsteps of her grandfather, her Aunt Isceola, and her mother. After completing grade school Violet June attended Texas College, Southeastern University, and Texas Southern University. Like her mother, her grandfather, and her aunt, she obtained teaching credentials and added to the commitment of this family of educators. She taught school for a number of years in the rural community of La Donia, Texas.

Walter Potts, Jr.
(date unknown).

G. B. Potts,
Military Police,
United States Army,
1951.

The first son, Walter Jr., was born on January 25, 1925. The solid family structure that Walter Jr. and Violet June experienced and lived in as children and their parents' love and appreciation for each other were essential parts of their upbringing. In 1944 Walter Jr. married Corine Steen Safford, the author's mother. The family grew quickly. LaVanda Jean was their first child, a daughter born on December 18, 1946. Their first son, Walter III, was born May 20, 1948. Another precious child, a son named Billy Ray, was born November 9, 1949. After the following year, Eva (the author) was born on May 16, 1951, honored with her dear grandmother's name. Walter Jr. died when Eva was a child. Janice Ann was Walter Jr. and Corine's last child. She was born on December 22, 1952. (The children were later blessed to have a dear stepfather, Henry, a brother, Maurice, and a beloved sister, Shree.)

G. B. was the last child born to Walter and Eva, on June 28, 1928. This made the family of Walter and Eva Potts complete. The three children enjoyed a pleasing childhood together. They went to school together. After college G. B. joined the army and served with the Military Police. He married Joye McNeal of Denison in October 1954. G. B. maintained a respected career as a successful businessman in Palo Alto, California, for many years. His business and community involvement were recognized statewide. He and Joye retired in Waller, Texas. (G. B. was instrumental in helping to put the information together for this book.)

Walter and Eva did not want any more children for their family. It may have been considered too small by the standards of some people because the family size during this time generally included six to eight children. As a busy father, Walter established a business as a blacksmith. He built the shop using his outstanding skills as a carpenter. The business flourished for a number of years. Walter was so skilled that he had only to see an object and he could duplicate it. He was always proud of that. His expertise was sought by many in the community. He always went back to the old farm to help his Grandfather Fountain at harvest time to help with gathering the crops. Everyone in the community helped each other. He boasted about their independence when he said that they did

THE WHITE HOUSE

WASHINGTON

January 6, 1995

Mr. Walter Edward Potts, Sr.
2169 San Rafael Avenue
Santa Clara, California 95051-1609

Dear Mr. Potts:

Happy 103rd Birthday! Hillary and I
wish you a memorable celebration, and we
hope that the coming year brings you great
happiness and good health.

Sincerely,

Bill Clinton

Above: *Birthday honor received from President Clinton.*

Below: *Walter E. Potts, Ruby Flowers, and friends,
100th birthday celebration, 1992.*

Walter E. Potts, May 1994, age 102. This photograph was featured on the Willard Scott birthday segment of NBC's Today Show on Walter's 103rd birthday, January 9, 1995.

Walter E. Potts, 1994.

not often have to make the long trip into town. Just about everything they needed was either on the farm or at one of the neighbors' home, farm, or business. Violet June remembered that Eva used to can all of their food. An abundance of chicken was fried and put up in one-gallon jars. The jars of chicken were then stored in the cellar. Fruits and vegetables were also canned. Watermelon rind preserves served as jam. The juice of a watermelon was also sometimes used for certain kidney ailments.

The business success enabled Walter to achieve his dream and enjoy the protection of owning a home for his family. Blacks who were engaged in business were important because of their social and political influence, as well as the economic strength they wielded. Although they felt the effects of the Great Depression, the Potts family did enjoy many other material things that were not available to others during that time.

When asked about race relations, Walter said, "At one time we were about the only blacks in our community. Folks I was brought up with were my brothers, no ifs ands or buts about it. We treated each other with respect and there was no difference made."

At the well-organized centenary birthday celebration, Walter was honored many times over by the attendees. This tribute came from LeRoy Lewis:

HAPPY 100TH BIRTHDAY

God gave us knowledge and courage without our asking,
then he gave us wisdom, strength, and serenity too.
For those things we should be forever grateful,
but today mostly we thank him for giving us you.
I have sat patiently many times listening to your words.
To a younger generation that might seem somewhat odd,
but they should learn one thing I did learn from you,
we will only get to where you are only by the grace of God.
I am sure that some roads you traveled were very long,
not to mention being tedious and often very rough.
Maybe God never gave you everything you wanted,

but your being here today means he gave you just enough.
Sometimes I searched and searched for answers,
but seemingly none would come my way.
I wondered out loud why God did not help.
He answered back, because you did not pray.
I try to learn from my past mistakes.
So I received what I have asked for on this day.
So one reason we have made it to this occasion,
is because this time I did remember to pray.

Ruby Flowers, another longtime friend, wrote this tribute
in honor of Walter's ninety-seventh birthday:

We Thank You
Your outstanding contributions to the community
has helped to bring us where we are today.
Whatever you were called on to do for us
you did it and we thank you.
As you moved about in our community and your church
quiet like with dignity and tact.
When we needed courage and strength,
not only in words but in action too,
you gave it and we thank you.
Our love for you cannot be put in print.
Although you are not as active as before.
But knowing you as we do we are sure that you
will be with us to see us through.
You will do it and we thank you.

Epilogue

This book is a tribute to Walter E. Potts. Walter, who celebrated his 105th birthday January 9, 1997, before his death that year on June 13, will always be known as a person of great character and wisdom. His love for humanity touched many lives. Most of all, his love of family and friends inspired him. For this book, he agreed to share a few words of wisdom that he gathered throughout his 105 years.

Annually, the congregation of Union Baptist Church in Ravenna is host to a Memorial Day service. That service in 1994 held special meaning for the Potts family. But first, a short history of the church is in order.

Union Baptist is the uniting of two churches in Ravenna. After the Emancipation Proclamation was signed, the wheels were set in motion to free all slaves. In 1870 a group of people in the northern part of the community organized a small country church. The name of that first church was Siloam.

Siloam Baptist Church had a humble beginning. A few black families gathered and organized the church in the Mulberry School District. It was a one-room log building. The Rev-

Walter E. Potts, 1996.

erend L. Borns was the pastor. The church grew spiritually and prospered. The large membership prompted the decision to build a new church in 1892. The site of that first church is one and a half miles from the present site of Union Baptist Church. This edifice was completed and dedicated in May 1894.

Over the years the population diminished, and in 1950 a very small, overworked congregation was found in distress. Meanwhile, Belfountain, the neighboring church, was also in distress. Belfountain Church had been organized in 1882. Reverend F. D. Johnson was the pastor. Both churches, with few members, made a decision to unite in order to survive.

In 1954, with much prayer, faith, and commitment, both churches united, and Union Baptist Church became the new name. Brother Robert L. Childress and Sister Maud Anna Childress named the church. The Reverend D. Berry was the pastor. The Siloam building is now the auditorium. The classrooms and pastor's office came from Belfountain.

The church membership has increased from twenty-eight in 1982 to more than fifty today. Reverend Charles L. Gent has been the pastor since September 11, 1982.

Walter Potts was designated the Honorary Father of Union Baptist Church. In a moving presentation, during the Memorial Day Service on May 1, 1994, Reverend Gent presented him with a commemorative souvenir book. It was the first time in three years that Walter had felt up to getting dressed and going to the church service. I was very honored to have the opportunity to visit the historic place. My grandfather, Walter, wanted to show me the church personally. He also wanted to introduce me to some of his friends, and some of the relatives that I had not met before.

Arnold, one longtime friend whom Walter referred to as a young one, was aged ninety-two. Another cheerful woman, Pauline Topsy Fitzgerald, was still very fond of Walter. I was especially proud to meet Emmitt Parker, my father's best friend when they were growing up. Time did not permit the visitation of the three cemeteries that are in the area. Fountain and Patsy Oliphant are buried in one of the cemeteries. Walter could not recall the illness that his grandfather died from, but he remembered that his grandfather suffered for ten long years before he died. Many other relatives are also buried in the cemetery at Ravenna.

Water-logged ground from the previous weeks of rain-storms and tornadoes made the dirt and rock road very soggy. It was not possible to reach the property on which the old home and farm were once located. The feeling of it once being a stone's throw from us was very meaningful. I knew that I was in a special location. My grandfather talked about some of the crops that he, his brother, and his grandfather grew. Wheat, hay, alfalfa, corn, and cotton grew very well in the area as well as a wide variety of vegetables. Some of the harvested crops were sold to the local residents and merchants, both black and white. The farm was in operation from dawn to dusk, and most of the time everyone worked as long as the day. All during the year, the soil and crops were carefully mon-itored. The animals were attended to and their food supplies were frequently checked to see that there was always an ade-quate supply available.

Once in a while my grandfather went fishing alone when there was time for some much needed relaxation. One of the several lakes located nearby is Bonham Lake, a 1,020-acre lake located on Timber Creek four miles north of Bonham.

Lake Texoma was one of Walter's favorite fishing spots. Fishing at the lake is some of the best in nation. Popular species include catfish, crappie, walleye, largemouth buffalo, and ten species of bass. The lake is a huge reservoir that spreads over 89,000 acres of Texas and Oklahoma. It is the impoundment of the Red River. With a shoreline of 580 miles, the lake includes innumerable scenic coves and inlets.

My grandfather would go fishing alone to have the oppor-tunity to reflect on his life. On occasion he just sat there by himself to try to ease the pain of the loss of his family that he undoubtedly felt. He had a life in which he was surrounded by many relatives at the farm. When he went fishing, Walter could think things through. Each time he lost a family mem-ber, somehow he was made stronger by the loss—from the passing of his two siblings, when he was a youngster, to the painful death of his mother and sister that he witnessed.

Walter E. Potts realized that his fortune in life was his life. He would devote the rest of his life to the service of others. He never forgot the consolations and the morals that he was fortunate enough to receive from his family.

Endnotes

1. Hondon B. Hargrove, *Buffalo Soldiers in Italy*, 2.
2. Ibid., 1-2.
3. William H. Leckie, *The Buffalo Soldiers*, 258-259.
4. Ibid., 63.
5. The Assistant Adjutant General, Department of Texas, to Shafter, June 30, 1875, Selected Letters Received Relating to Texas, 187-1876, Adjutant General's Office, National Archives.
6. Leckie, 147-148.
7. Capt. S.B.M. Young to the Acting Assistant Adjutant General, District of the Nueces, December 18, 1877, File No. 1653; Lieutenant Bullis to the Post Adjutant, Fort Clark, Texas, December 22, 1877.
8. United States Congress, House. H. R. Exec. Doc. No. 1, Part 2, 45 Cong., 2 Sess., 49.
9. William Loren Katz, *The Black West*, 272-273.
10. U.S. Office of the Deputy Assistant Secretary of Defense for Civilian Personnel Policy Equal Opportunity, Department of Defense, *Black Americans in Defense of Our Nation*, 49.
11. Charles Williams, *Negro Soldiers in World War I: The Human Side,* formerly titled: *Sidelights on Negro Soldiers,* 22-23.
12. Ibid.
13. U.S. Office of the Deputy Assistant Secretary of Defense for Civilian Personnel Policy Equal Opportunity, Department of Defense, *Black Americans in Defense of Our Nation*, p. 50-53.
14. Ibid.

15. Jesse J. Johnson, *A Pictorial History of Black Soldiers in the United States (1619-1969)*, p. 36

16. NA Record Group No. 407; *Unit History, Battalion War Diary*, Adjutant General Office Reports of Foreign Service Records Orders. form No. 491.

17. Bernard C. Nalty, *Strength for the Fight: A History of Black Americans in the Military,* 115.

18. NA Record Group No. 407; *Unit History, Battalion War Diary*, Adjutant General Office Reports of Foreign Service Records Orders. form No. 491.

19. Ibid.

20. Ibid.

21. *Pictorial History, Three Hundred Sixty Seventh Infantry, Army of the United States.* U.S. Army Military History Institute, 1942, 9.

22. Arthur E. Barbeau and Florette Henri, *The Unknown Soldiers: Black American Troops in World War I*, 84.

23. Addie W. Hunton and Kathryn Johnson, *Two Colored Women With the American Expeditionary Forces*, 52.

24. Williams, *Negro Soldiers in World War I*, 157-158.

25. Osceola McKaine, "The Buffaloes," *Outlook* 119 (22 May 1918):146.

26. Hunton and Johnson, 182.

27. Ibid., 188.

28. Ibid., 197.

29. *New York Times*, February 18, 1919, 1.

30. Bernard C. Nalty, *Strength for the Fight: A History of Black Americans in the Military*, 117, 118.

31. Barbeau and Henri, 160.

32. Williams, *Negro Soldiers in World War I*, 169-170.

33. Stanley Weintraub, *A Stillness Heard Round the World: The End of the Great War*, November 1918, 100, 101.

34. Barbeau and Henri, 121.

35. Williams, *Negro Soldiers in World War I*, 205.

36. Hunton and Johnson, 51.

37. Ibid., 54-55.

38. *New York Times,* February 18, 1919, 1.

39. Barbeau and Henri, 171.

40. Ibid.

41. John Hope Franklin, *From Slavery To Freedom: A History of Negro Americans,* Fifth Edition, 334.

42. Ibid., 334, 335.

43. D. B. Hardeman and Donald Bacon, *Rayburn: A Biography*, 47.

44. Ibid., 333.

45. Richard Bolling, *House Out of Order*, 174, 177.

46. Hardeman and Bacon, 418.

47. *Congressional Record*, June 8, 1956, 8914, 8915, 8916.

48. Anthony Champange, *Congressman Sam Rayburn*, 12-13.

49. Hardeman and Bacon, 431.

Bibliography

BOOKS

Barbeau, Arthur E., and Florette Henri. *The Unknown Soldiers: Black American Troops in World War I.* Philadelphia: Temple University Press, 1974.

Bolling, Richard. *House Out of Order.* New York: E. P. Dutton and Co., 1965.

Champange, Anthony. *Congressman Sam Rayburn.* New Brunswick: Rutgers University Press, 1984.

Dowd, Jerome. *The Negro in American Life.* New York: Century, 1926.

Franklin, John Hope. *From Slavery to Freedom: A History of Negro Americans: Fifth Edition.* New York: Alfred A. Knopf, Inc., 1980.

Hardeman, D. B., and Donald Bacon. *Rayburn A Biography.* Austin: Texas Monthly Press, Inc. 1987.

Hargrove, Hondon B. *Buffalo Soldiers in Italy: Black Americans in World War II.* North Carolina: McFarland and Company, Inc., 1985.

Hunton, Addie W., and Kathryn M. Johnson. *Two Colored Women With The American Expeditionary Forces.* New York: AMS Press, 1971.

Johnson, Jesse J. *A Pictorial History of Black Soldiers in the United States (1619-1969).* Hampton: Hampton Institute, 1970.

Katz, William Loren. *The Black West: A Pictorial History, Third Edition, Revised and Expanded.* Seattle: Open Hand Publishing Inc., 1987.

Leckie, William H. *The Buffalo Soldiers: A Narrative of the Negro Cavalry in the West.* Oklahoma: University of Oklahoma Press, 1967.

Little, Arthur W. *From Harlem to the Rhine: The Story of New York's Colored Volunteers.* New York: Corvici Friede, 1936.

Nalty, Bernard C. *Strength for the Fight: A History of Black Americans in the Military.* New York: The Free Press, 1986.

Sweeney, W. Allison. *History of the American Negro in the Great World War.* Chicago: Cueno, Henneberry, 1919.

U.S. Office of the Deputy Assistant Secretary of Defense for Civilian Personnel Policy, Equal Opportunity, Department of Defense. *Black Americans in Defense of our Nation.* Washington, DC: Government Printing Office, 1991.

Weintraub, Stanley. *A Stillness Heard Round The World: The End of the Great War.* New York: Trauman Talley Books, E. P. Dutton, 1985.

Williams, Charles. *Negro Soldiers in World War I: The Human Side, formerly titled: Sidelights on Negro Soldiers.* New York: AMS Press, Inc., 1970.

———. *Sidelights on Negro Soldiers.* Boston: Brimmer, 1923.

NEWSPAPERS

New York Times, 18 February 1919.
New York Times, 23 February 1919, section 5.

PERIODICALS

McKaine, Osceola. "The Buffaloes." *Outlook,* May 1918, 146.

GOVERNMENT PAPERS

Irvin, Helen B. U.S. Department of Labor, Division of Negro Economics. Washington, DC: 1919.

National Archives, Record Group 94. Assistant Adjutant General, Department of Texas. Selected Letters Received Relating to Texas, 1875, 1876. Washington, DC.

National Archives Record Group No. 407. *Unit History, Battalion War Diary.* Washington, DC: Adjutant General Office Reports of Foreign Service Records and Orders, form No. 491.

Pictorial History, Three Hundred Sixty Seventh Infantry, Army of the United States. U.S. Army Military History Institute, 1942.

The Ninety Second Division, 1917/1918: An Analytical Study. Washington Barracks, DC: Army War College, 1923.

The Papers of Woodrow Wilson. Edited by Arthur Link (36:4-19, 26-48, 52-73, 75-85, 87-122, 41:519-27) by volume and page number.

U.S. American Battle Monuments Commission. *92d Division: Summary of Operations in the World War.* Washington, DC: Government Printing Office, 1944.

U.S. Army Special Information Section. *Headquarters Army Ground Forces.* Washington, DC: U.S. Office of Technical Information, 1945.

U.S. Army, War College. *Colored Soldiers in the U.S. Army.* Washington, DC: Government Printing Office, 1942.

U.S. War Department. *General Orders, No. 11*. Washington, DC: Government Printing Office, 1924.

U.S. War Department. *The Official Record of the United States' Part in the Great War*. Washington, DC: Government Printing Office, 1923.

War Department. *Annual Reports, 1916*. Washington, DC: Government Printing Office, 1917.

SPECIAL COLLECTIONS, PUBLISHED AND UNPUBLISHED

Reedy, Lloyd M., and Edward H. Phillips. *The Origin of Pottsboro*. Pottsboro: 1993.

St. Clair, Kathleen E., and Clifton R. St. Clair. *Little Towns of Texas*. Jacksonville: Jayroe Graphic Arts, Inc., 1982.

Webb, Walter Prescott, ed. *The Handbook of Texas, Volume 1*. Austin: Texas State Historical Association, 1952.

Index